convection cookery

convection cookery

caroline kriz

illustrations by
bill oetinger

101 productions
san francisco

Published by 101 Productions
834 Mission Street
San Francisco, California 94103

Distributed to the book trade in the United States by
Charles Scribner's Sons, New York.

Library of Congress Cataloging in Publication Data

Kriz, Caroline.
    Convection cookery.

    Includes index.
    1.   Convection oven cookery.   I. Title.
TX840.C65K74   641.5'8   80-19915
ISBN 0-89286-181-9

contents

introduction
to convection cooking

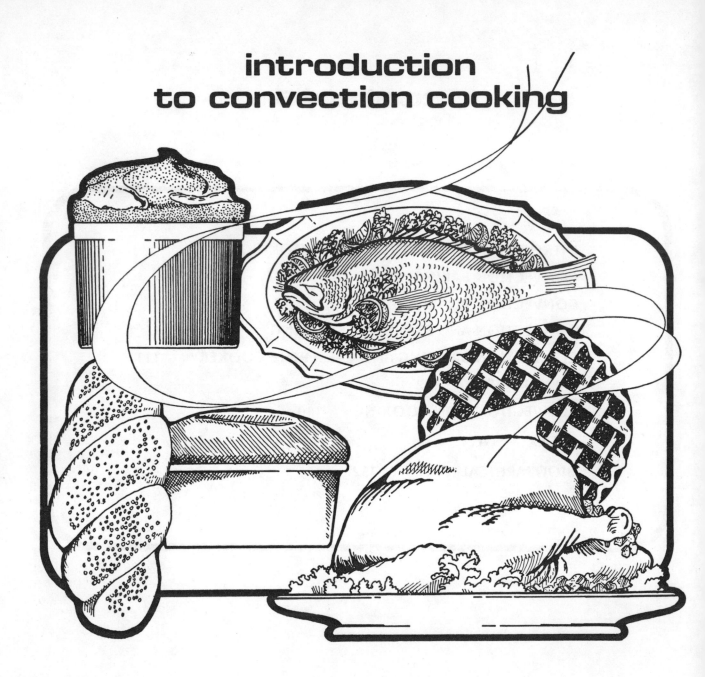

WHAT IS CONVECTION COOKING?

The question "What is convection cooking?" has a very simple answer: It is the process of oven cooking by circulating hot air. So simple is this description that many people who hear it become instant skeptics. They cannot believe the claims and accolades of manufacturers and convection devotees that circulating hot air can make a big difference in food quality and cooking time. They cannot believe it, that is, until they have tried it.

I first encountered convection cooking in 1977 while taking lessons with the *grande dame* of French cuisine, Simone Beck. There in Simca's kitchen in her charming La Campanette (Teaching House) was a built-in oven that looked like any other oven I had ever seen. Out of it came the most scrumptious treats: crispy pastries, voluminous soufflés, succulent meats. It was only after a couple of days of gorging myself with samples of Simca's masterpieces that I stopped chomping long enough to hear the difference. That's right, I *heard* the difference between a convection oven and a standard oven before I saw it. There was a gentle humming coming from the oven, which I discovered was the fan that every convection oven has. Reduced to its most basic terms, it is this fan that turns a conventional oven into a convection oven.

Upon returning to the United States from that trip, I found myself teaching my "Cooking For Men Only" classes in a test kitchen with a convection oven, among others. I loved it for its speed and efficiency, but unfortunately I could not use it often without confusing my students, who were just warming up to the concept of plain old "oven."

I had learned on my trip to France that convection ovens were in widespread use both in restaurants and homes throughout Europe. Soon after, I was asked to demonstrate one of the new crop of portable convection ovens coming into the marketplace at the Chicago Housewares Show. That prolonged firsthand experience convinced me that convection cooking has a place in almost every American kitchen.

Convincing a skeptic like me was no small task. As a freelance food consultant and former magazine editor and consumer adviser, I was (and still am) flabbergasted by the number of small portable appliances available to the American consumer.

Once, as I was about to step into a radio studio to do a show on "What's New in Housewares," I made a list of no less than 22 portable appliances in less than 60 seconds! Twenty-two portable appliances flowed from the tip of my pen without even a second thought! The list ranged from toasters to irons to popcorn poppers to hot dog cookers. I asked myself: "With our diminishing space, increasing apartment living and rising real estate costs, where are we supposed to store all these kitchen helpers?" The answer is obvious: We are not supposed to store all of them. As consumers we must be brutally selective in our housewares purchases. If an appliance does not save time, make our work easier and clean up quickly, it doesn't deserve to be purchased.

My experience with portable convection ovens has shown me that they fill these requirements. They do save cooking time due to their efficient heating; they make work easier because the natural searing action means we don't have to baste or otherwise tend most foods; and they are, for the most part, designed for easy care.

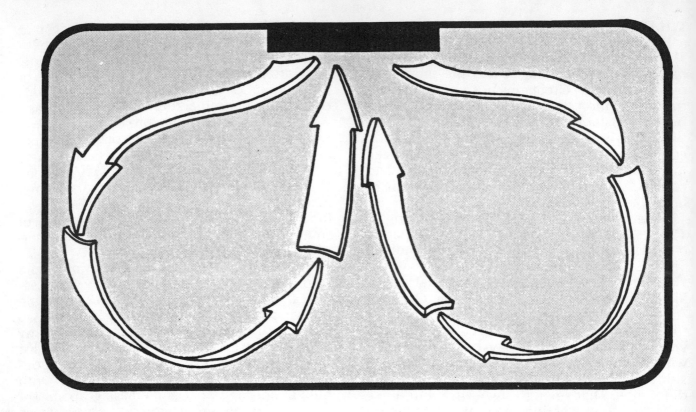

WHAT MAKES CONVECTION COOKING DIFFERENT?

When you first try convection cooking, what are the differences you will encounter? You'll find that countertop convection ovens
● cook foods up to one third faster than conventional ovens.
● sear meats and poultry quickly, sealing in juices and eliminating the need for basting.
● brown evenly and from all sides.
● cost less to buy than built-in ovens and perform all the tasks you expect of an oven.

● are portable, can be plugged into any standard outlet and can be moved from the kitchen to the family room or summer home with ease. (Manufacturers do not recommend using countertop convection ovens outdoors.)

For a complete roundup of convection advantages, see page 11.

Without even realizing it, most Americans have experienced convection cooking. Convection ovens have been in use in American restaurants for several years now. Chances are if you have eaten a juicy prime rib cooked to just the right degree of doneness, or a delicately broiled

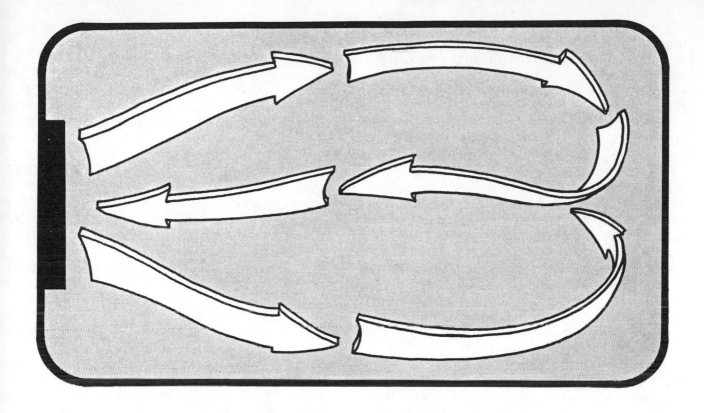

fish or a high and handsome dessert soufflé at your favorite restaurant, it was cooked in a convection oven.

The models used by restaurants, of course, are large built-in institutional ovens. While they look different than countertop convection ovens, hold large quantities and cost much more, the cooking principle is the same: to bake, roast, broil and braise food by surrounding it on all sides by forced hot air. The air is heated by an element, circulated by a fan throughout the oven cavity, then drawn back toward the fan, heated and circulated again. This pattern of circulating air is called "air flow."

DIRECTION OF AIR FLOW: DOES IT MATTER?

Different brands of countertop convection ovens approach the design of air-flow patterns in different ways. There are basically two types of air flow:

1. up-and-down air flow that results from placement of the fan in the *top wall* of the oven.

2. side-to-side air flow that results from placement of the fan in the *side wall or rear wall* of the oven. (Rear wall fans actually force air from back to front but the result is basically the same as side-to-side air flow.)

There are differences between cooking in a top-wall fan model and a side-wall fan model, but they are not so extreme that one can be recommended over the other. After extensive testing, I have found that the differences between the two are concentrated mainly in the baking mode. These differences won't be crucial to the cook who uses the oven primarily for roasting and broiling.

TOP-FAN MODELS

● brown the tops of baked goods beautifully but sometimes too quickly, which may result in undercooked bottoms. One way to remedy this is to place the food on the bottom rack of the oven. Another remedy is to lower the temperature setting and adjust the baking time.

● do not bake the bottom layer of foods as quickly as the top layer when baking on two levels with two baking sheets. The top sheet tends to shield the bottom one. This can be remedied by allowing the bottom sheet to bake a few minutes longer than the top one.

● may cook or brown foods more quickly than side-fan models, especially if the heating element is *in* the oven cavity as is the case with certain models. To remedy, decrease cooking time and/or reduce temperature by 25 degrees.

SIDE-FAN MODELS

● tend to create fast-browning spots on baked goods positioned close to the fan when bakeware is close to oven walls. Sometimes the spot develops opposite the fan and results from the forced hot air reflecting off the far wall. To remedy fast-browning spots, use bakeware that is the proper size for your oven and turn items once or twice during baking just as you would in a standard oven. You may also wish to turn down the oven temperature and increase the baking time.

● may not brown the center top of large flat baked goods as quickly as they brown the edges due to side-to-side air flow. To remedy, reduce the oven temperature and increase the baking time.

WHY BUY A CONVECTION OVEN ANYWAY?

If you are considering buying a second (or third) oven for your home, it is wise to consider buying a countertop convection oven for any of the following reasons:

● If you wish to add another oven to your kitchen without the expense of remodeling or installing another built-in oven. Convection ovens are reasonable in price, with suggested retail prices ranging from $100 to $300, with sale prices sometimes available.

● If you cook for a meat-and-potatoes family. Nothing compares to convection-roasted meats for time savings and quality. Braising recipes are substantial time and energy savers, too.

● If you have never been convinced that microwave-cooked foods and microwave ovens are for you and your life style. Convection ovens offer an alternative that is not as fast as microwave but is faster than conventional ovens, and results that look and taste the way you are used to.

● If you need an oven that can be moved easily for "special duty"—into the family room for a teenage party, to a neighbor's house for a potluck dinner or to a vacation cottage for the summer season.

ADVANTAGES OF CONVECTION COOKING

Any one of the following advantages may be sufficient cause to become a convection devotee. But cooks don't have to settle for just one. They will find the following true of all countertop convection ovens:

● **Convection-Cooked Foods Are Juicier and More Moist.** The circulating hot air sears meats and poultry quickly to seal in natural juices. This minimizes shrinkage, which helps stretch the consumer meat dollar. This same action helps baked goods retain moisture and rise quickly.

● **Convection Ovens Cook An Average of One Third Faster Than Standard Gas or Electric Ovens.** The time savings varies with modes of cooking and with individual recipes. With some recipes time savings is as high as 50 percent; with others, as low as 20 percent. Time savings are greatest and most consistent when roasting and braising. When baking, time savings fluctuate depending upon the depth, richness and moisture content of the batter or dough. A cheesecake, for example, may not bake in reduced time. Due to its rich, moist batter, it may take the full standard time to bake all the way through without over-browning the top or sides. It is very difficult to dry out a cheesecake or similar item in a countertop convection oven.

● **Convection Ovens Brown Evenly.** The circulating air browns from all sides, including the bottom. The appearance of convection-cooked foods is picture perfect.

● **Convection Ovens Save Energy and Energy Dollars.** Depending on the model, countertop convection ovens operate on 1,200 to 1,500 watts, while a typical electric oven operates on about 3,000 watts. Varying savings may occur over standard gas ovens depending upon the comparative energy costs between gas and electricity in any given geographic area. The additional energy is saved due to reduced cooking times.

● **Convection Ovens Utilize Typical Bakeware or No Bakeware at All.** Special bakeware is not needed for convection cooking. Cake pans, baking sheets, roasting pans and casseroles that are used for standard cooking can be used in convection ovens. Often when broiling and roasting, no cooking utensil besides the oven rack and drip pan are needed. Aluminum and other metal bakeware is recommended by manufacturers, but glass and ceramic can be used. They may, however, not result in reduced cooking times.

● **Convection-Broiled Foods Cook on Both Sides at Once.** Convection broiling offers the cook the ease of broiling without turning foods over halfway through cooking. Searing broiler foods from both sides at once means natural juices are sealed in and "rare" and "medium rare" doneness is easy to achieve. (See the chapter on broiling, beginning on page 91.)

LIMITATIONS OF CONVECTION OVENS

A fair assessment of countertop convection ovens would not be complete without a discussion of their limitations.

● **Size—One Inch is the Key.** A countertop convection oven is, after all, a portable appliance. It naturally follows that it will not be large enough to hold everything that a built-in oven can hold. But it comes amazingly close to that capability. Manufacturers are quick to point out that a 12- to 17-pound turkey can be cooked in the countertop models (depending on the individual oven model). And it is true—all the space that's needed around any item is one inch all around. Even oven cavities that *look* small are surprisingly spacious.

But it is not so much *what* you cook in the oven as *how much* of it you wish to cook. Those items that cannot be cooked in the countertop models are those that will not fit into the oven with one inch of air space all around. These include large, high-breasted turkeys (check care-and-use manual for exact size); a full bone-in leg of lamb (sirloin and shank) over six to eight pounds; any item that has to be cooked on a baking sheet larger than the oven will accommodate, such as a 12-inch round pizza; a whole fish that's longer than the oven cavity (usually over four to five pounds); two of anything broad and high such as bundt cakes or braided breads; any Dutch oven that won't fit in the oven cavity.

The recipes that follow have been developed with the size limitations of portable convection ovens in mind. The Houska recipe on page 33, for example, will fit into any size convection oven available. If you double the recipe and make two loaves, they can be baked side by side in those ovens with larger cavities. When the phrase "to fit oven" is used in describing bakeware, it means any size bakeware can be used as long as it fits into the oven with at least one inch of air space between the bakeware and the oven wall.

● **Super-Rich Baked Goods May Not Cook Properly.** While many rich baked foods can be baked successfully in countertop ovens, (several are included in the "Baking" chapter), you may sometime encounter a baking recipe that will not cook properly because of the high moisture or fat content. If lowering the temperature and increasing baking time does not work, try adjusting the recipe by decreasing liquid or chocolate or cream—whatever ingredient makes the recipe rich. If that still does not give you a topnotch product, make this recipe one of those you bake only in your conventional oven.

● **Convection Broiling is Not the Same as Standard Broiling.** Anyone who is wild for standard-broiled foods may not be happy with convection-broiled foods. On the other hand, many may like convection-broiled foods better. The difference is that the convection-broiled items do not get as charred or crusty on the outside as standard-broiled items. They are tender inside and retain some tenderness on the outside. See the chapter on broiling, beginning on page 91, for more on this cooking method.

TO PREHEAT OR NOT TO PREHEAT? THAT IS THE QUESTION

On the question of whether or not to preheat convection ovens, I disagree with much of the promotional rhetoric that claims preheating is unnecessary. In my view, convection ovens (as well as conventional ovens) should be preheated, especially for baked goods. Baking, more than any other type of cooking, relies for success on a recipe that is in essence a chemical formula. Just as the right number of eggs in a soufflé or the proper amount of flour in a bread is essential to success, so is the temperature at which that food is cooked. Temperature is too crucial to most recipes to be treated carelessly. Quick, high heat, for example, is what makes a soufflé rise straight up without the support of an aluminum foil collar and what sears meats so that they retain natural juices.

Basically, my objection to placing foods in a cold oven is that it becomes much more difficult to time the cooking accurately. Certain variables are created in a cold oven situation that are not conducive to accurate timing. For one, the temperature of the food entering the oven can vary drastically. One day you may roast meat straight from the refrigerator, while another day the meat may stay out at room temperature for some time before going into the oven. Some cooks like to bake pastry doughs as soon as they are assembled; others will refrigerate them first, still others will pop them in the freezer (which usually makes for a better product). There can also be a difference of 10 to 15 degrees in the "cold" oven temperature depending upon the room temperature of the kitchen. Still another variable is that different ovens heat to selected temperatures at different rates. This is not just true from brand to brand but also from oven to oven within a brand. This is a matter of fact with any appliance that operates on a thermostat.

The variation of food and oven-start temperatures combined with varying heat-up rates makes for fluctuating cooking times. And that's too uncertain for me. Through my testing I have found I get more uniform, consistently good results when I preheat the oven. The natural searing or "seizing" action that is an integral advantage of convection cooking does not have a chance to work when you begin cooking with a cold oven. I recommend that convection ovens be preheated for baking, broiling and braising. Preheating could be eliminated when roasting since a meat thermometer, and not time alone, indicates doneness. But I still prefer the searing action that takes place when roasts are thrust into a hot oven.

The case for preheating convection ovens is not upheld by me alone. In my studies with Simca in the South of France, at La Varenne in Paris and with various celebrated food authorities here in the United States, I have never encountered a truly talented chef putting food in a cold convection oven. And time and time again I, as a student, have been cautioned to make sure my oven is preheated to the correct temperature. Preheating is not absolutely necessary; it simply makes for a better product. In a way, it is like pastry dough: When it's made with margarine, it's OK. When it's made with butter, it is superb! Not preheating and preheating is the difference between OK and superb.

Note: If your oven's care-and-use manual does not give preheat times but you wish to preheat, use the following times:

5 minutes for temperatures up to 300°F
10 minutes for 325°F to 375°F
15 minutes for 400°F and over

REHEATING IN A CONVECTION OVEN

Reheating foods of all sorts is quick and efficient in a convection oven. The biggest advantage is that convection heat tends not to dry out foods as it reheats. Foods can be reheated wrapped snugly or loosely in aluminum foil or without any wrapping at all.

Foods you do not wish to brown further, such as a slice of pizza or a piece of broiled meat, should be wrapped in aluminum foil before reheating. Casseroles that will not benefit from further browning should be covered tightly with foil also. Foods you wish to brown or crisp, such as rolls and pastries, can be placed directly on the oven rack without wrapping.

Set the temperature control at 275°F or 300°F except when a recipe gives special reheating directions. Reheating times generally range from five to 20 minutes depending on the size and thickness of the item and on how hot the item must be for serving. Reheating rolls to warm will of course take less time than reheating a refrigerated casserole to piping hot.

Convection ovens do not have to be preheated for reheating; however, preheating does make timing more accurate, which helps eliminate overcooking during reheating.

A WORD ABOUT RECIPES

The recipes in this book have been developed specifically for countertop convection ovens. Each of them has been tested in a convection oven at least once, many of them in two or three different models. They are intended as delicious guidelines to the world of convection cookery. Each recipe gives suggested bakeware and standard oven temperature and time so the recipes are not restricted to convection use. While I am not one to stifle a creative cook, I advise that when trying a recipe for the first time you cook it as it is written. Next time around, after you have seen how the recipe reacts and what the timing is, you can make modifications if you so choose.

The recipes I have developed for convection ovens are a result of my formal culinary training and the culinary common sense I learned at my mother's knee. In addition, my experience as a magazine editor has given me an insight into what American cooks want in their recipe collections: On a day-to-day basis, simplicity and wholesomeness are the main considerations.

But when entertaining, hosts and hostesses don't mind spending extra time and money and using richer foods to do something special.

To help cooks make selections quickly and easily, many of the recipes that follow are coded. This symbol ○ denotes a "quick-and-easy" recipe—one with fast total preparation time or with fast pre-oven preparation time that frees the cook to do other things. This symbol ☆ denotes recipes that you'll want to reserve for special occasions due to complexity and/or cost. They are ideal for entertaining guests or for family celebrations. Recipes with no symbol are somewhere in between these two categories in timing, complexity and expense.

You won't find a great many convenience foods in these recipes except for relatively unadulterated ones such as frozen fruits and vegetables, because of my belief that fresh is best. Simple frozen foodstuffs that capture freshness at its peak—such as frozen spinach, green beans or peaches—are a boon to modern cooks. But contrived frozen foods—such as hot dog sandwiches and pre-cooked pancakes—are expensive, low-quality contrivances that are an insult to homemakers and shoppers everywhere. How long does it take to pop a hot dog into a convection oven, place it on a bun and garnish it with fresh condiments? About as long as it takes to heat a frozen hot dog sandwich and with no sacrifice in flavor and quality.

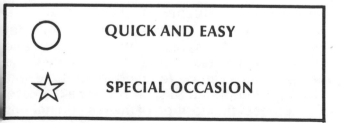

	QUICK AND EASY
	SPECIAL OCCASION

ON GROCERY SHOPPING

Consumers are constantly advised on "how to save money in the supermarket." I myself toured the country in 1978 offering suggestions and information on this topic, which is so important to family budgeting. I will not repeat all the clues to money-saving shopping here. I do want to offer, however, a suggestion I rarely hear but firmly believe: Get to know your grocer!

Making friends with your grocer may not result in immediate savings, but it will result in better eating for your family and in reduced grocery bills in the long run. The manager, butcher and greengrocer of your favorite supermarket can give you insights into shopping and offer you recourse should you ever be dissatisfied with a product.

Several years ago I quite accidentally met George Kamberos, the proud owner of a chain of independent supermarkets that have built a glowing reputation by stocking a most marvelous array of ethnic foods, all neatly grouped by country of origin, as well as the standard broad array of supermarket foodstuffs. George was happy to answer my questions and was pleased to be asked. Now if I ever have a grocery question, I call George and he's quick with the answer. And what I have learned from George just chatting with him over the kiwi fruit and Cranshaw melons! His 50 years, man and boy, in the grocery business has made *me* a better shopper. Of course, he doesn't stop and chat with every shopper in his nine stores—just with those who express interest and ask questions. That goes for grocery people in general. They want to answer your questions and help you make intelligent selections. So get to know your grocer!

FUNCTIONS, FEATURES AND WHAT TO LOOK FOR

Every countertop convection oven on the market is the ideal choice for someone, but they are not all right for everyone. If you are thinking of buying a countertop convection oven for your own use or as a gift, you should be aware of the various styles and features available before making a decision. The ovens on the market vary in function, size and design. Each model has strengths and weaknesses, depending upon what you expect from your convection oven.

THE BASICS

VERSATILITY—DO YOU NEED IT?
Some models are strictly convection ovens. Forced air heating is all they do and they do it well. Other models are more versatile. They may be combination convection-microwave ovens or include a standard broiling element or have a setting for regular radiant oven heat or may have a low setting for dehydrating. (For more on dehydrating, see the "Non-Cooking" chapter beginning on page 140.) Think of the way you cook now and try to match the oven to your style. If you are currently doing a great deal of broiling, you may want an oven that offers both convection and standard broiling. If speed is most important to you, check out the convection-microwave combinations. If your primary interest lies in roasting and baking, a single-function convection oven will fit the bill.

SIZE—CHECK INSIDE AND OUT
Size is an important consideration. Check both oven cavity size, which determines how much you can put in it, and overall size, which determines how much space it will take up in your kitchen. Remember to swing the oven door open to see how much additional cleared space you will need in front of the oven.

EASE OF USE
Countertop convection ovens are, on a whole, easy to use. They plug into standard outlets and are so similar to the conventional ovens we are used to that no new skills need to be learned—only new timings and approaches to old cooking skills. But there are certain questions to ask yourself when shopping for convection ovens, and they vary with individuals and their concerns.
● Can I open and close the oven door with one hand?
● Can I handle oven racks with one hand?
● Are the control knobs designed so that my short fingers can handle them easily? Even if my fingers are a little greasy?
● Will I be able to remove a hot drip pan easily when I wish to use drippings for gravy-making?
● When this oven is on my countertop, will I be able to read the controls easily?
● Do the racks have a stop on them so I won't accidentally pull one all the way out when it's holding a Dutch oven full of pot roast?

SINGLE-WALL VS. MULTIPLE-WALL
Some convection oven authorities consider oven-wall thickness of primary importance and believe that cooking times are reduced and temperatures can be reduced in multiple wall ovens. I do not find this always to be the case. Rather I feel the position of the fan and heating

element have the most effect on cooking time and temperature. Although it isn't always true, when there is a difference in cooking time between top-fan ovens and side-fan ovens, the top-fan ovens cook faster but not necessarily better. This is also true of ovens with the heating element in the oven cavity. They brown faster but do not necessarily cook better than ovens with the heating element housed in the oven wall.

The difference between single- and multiple-wall units is in the surface heat. Single-wall models tend to get hotter to the touch. Multiple-wall models do not get as hot, but some get hotter than others. Some multiple-wall models are insulated, others are not.

If this sounds confusing, it is good to remember one important (and very elementary) fact: Convection ovens get hot. They cook food (superbly) by heat, not by microwaves, which leave the oven cavity cool. During my experience demonstrating convection ovens at trade shows, I have encountered countless individuals who have confused convection with microwave. They slap their hands against the top or side of an operating convection oven, then quickly draw away and with an incredulous look say, "Wow! That's hot!" Not surprising when you consider the oven has been going full-tilt for the past five hours. Yes, convection ovens get hot.

Just as you would never think of resting your hand on or leaning up against a gas or electric oven while it is operating, you should not think of handling a convection oven, single or multiple wall, while it is operating except in the way prescribed in the care-and-use manual. With any model, it is a good idea to keep plastic bags away from the front of the unit while it is operating.

APPEARANCE

Countertop convection ovens vary greatly in their styling. Some have light-colored enameled surfaces, others are woodgrain. Some are very contemporary, others have a more conservative look. While styling should not be the primary reason for selecting an oven, it should be taken into consideration. Because a convection oven sits on the countertop and not behind closed doors, it becomes a part of your kitchen decor.

FEATURES

There are basically two types of features: universal features, which all or most ovens have, and special features, which are unique to certain models or are optional at additional cost. Here is a listing of what you'll find on the market, along with recommendations on what to look for. Don't be bashful when you are looking for an appliance. Look for a store that has a demonstrator model set up and handle it, if at all possible. Open and close the door, slide the racks in and out, turn the knobs, try to pick it up to check its weight. That is the best way to get a feel for what you like—and dislike.

UNIVERSAL FEATURES	WHAT TO LOOK FOR
Control Panel	Easy-to-handle knobs that are easy to reach
Timer	A timer that times long enough to roast meats and poultry without resetting and is easy to read, with a bell or buzzer to let you know when the timer turns off
Temperature Range	All ovens go up to the 450° to 475°F range, but only certain models go down to 150°F. If you wish to use your oven for dehydrating foodstuffs, look for a control that goes down to 140° to 150°F.
Heating Element	If the heating element is in the oven cavity, it will brown foods more quickly than if housed in the oven wall. It may be necessary to reduce temperature by 25 degrees when the heating element is in the cavity.
Racks and Rack Positions	If you will be using your oven frequently for baking or cooking several items at once, look for a model with two oven racks with multiple positions. (Extra oven racks are available separately through manufacturers.) If you plan on using your oven mainly for roasting, convection broiling and casseroles, one oven rack may be sufficient.
Door	A door that lets you see into the oven easily and can be removed and immersed for thorough cleaning. Some doors are dishwasher-safe, others are not.

UNIVERSAL FEATURES	WHAT TO LOOK FOR
Interior Oven Surface	A surface with continuous-clean material. Spatters will disintegrate to a powder and can be sponged off.
Oven Walls	Check to see if the unit is a single- or multiple-wall model. Single-wall models will get hotter to the touch.
Temperature Indicator Light	Available on some but not all models, this light lets you know when the selected temperature is reached and cycles off and on during cooking to show that the temperature is maintained. Some models have a light that goes on whenever the oven is operating, which is not nearly as helpful as a temperature indicator light. If you are in favor of preheating, this feature is very helpful.
Noise	All convection ovens make noise because there is a fan motor running all the while the oven is operating. There is a difference in noise levels from oven to oven. If possible, have the clerk plug in and run the demonstrator model, and listen carefully. What sounds soft to you in a busy housewares department may sound loud in your kitchen.
Filter	Some models include a filter that catches grease before it gets to the fan blades. There is no appreciable difference in cooking in filter or non-filter models. The filter is replaceable and may benefit the cleaning process in the long run.

SPECIAL FEATURES	DESCRIPTION
Standard Broiling	Included on some models at no extra cost to give the oven the dual capability of traditional broiling as well as convection broiling. See the "Broiling" chapter for more information.
Rotisserie	Standard on some models at no extra cost. If you like spit-roasted meats and poultry, you'll want to look for this feature. While convection roasting seals in juices, the rotating movement of the rotisserie creates internal self-basting for an extra-juicy and even result.
Shish Kabob Rack and Skewers	An optional extra on some models. The ideal way to cook kabobs in a convection oven is on a specially designed rack. Extra skewers let you cook some while filling others.
Dehydrating Racks	An optional extra on some models. Check the oven care-and-use manual to order dehydrating racks. A good feature to look for if you have a garden and wish to dry foods for use throughout the winter months. See the "Non-Cooking" chapter for more on dehydrating.
Slow Cook	Standard on some models at no extra cost. Allows you to use the convection oven as a slow cooker: turn it on in the morning and leave on low temperature setting all day. A good feature for the working cook who cooks braised dishes and casseroles. (The recipes in the "Braising" chapter are for regular convection cooking times, not slow-cooking times.)

SPECIAL FEATURES	DESCRIPTION
Light	Standard on some models; an optional extra on others. Good if you simply *must* see that back row of cookies. Eliminates the need to keep a flashlight near the oven or to open the door too often.
Stay-on Setting	Standard on some models at no extra cost. Allows the oven to stay on indefinitely. Usually used for "slow cooking" so oven timer does not have to be reset.
Temperature Probe	Standard on some models at no extra cost. When inserted in meat or poultry the probe automatically turns off the oven or signals when the desired internal temperature is reached. Usually on top-of-the-line models. You can get the same result using a meat thermometer but you won't get an automatic turn-off or a signal.
Delay Start Timer	Standard on some top-of-the-line models, optional on others. This feature can program the oven to turn on at a certain time of day so that cooking is completed even when the cook is out. (Similar to a feature found on top-of-the-line built-in ovens.)

convection
baking

CONVECTION BAKING

Baking is the most obvious and most frequently used function of any oven and that includes convection ovens. Cakes, pies, cookies, brownies and rolls can all be baked successfully in a convection oven. So can many of the more exotic baked items such as soufflés, quiches, brioches, puff pastry and custards. One reason many restaurant soufflés rise so beautifully is that they are baked in convection ovens.

Cooks should be careful not to fall prey to The Toaster Oven Syndrome when deciding on what to bake in their countertop convection ovens. What is The Toaster Oven Syndrome? Simply the notion that because an appliance is compact, sits on the counter and resembles a toaster oven it is best used like a toaster oven: restricted to baking convenience foods such as refrigerated rolls and frozen pies. Nothing could be further from the truth.

The recipes found later in this chapter attest to the versatility of convection baking. There is literally no baked product that cannot be baked in a convection oven as long as it has been properly modified and allows at least one inch of air space all around. There are, as you would expect, certain differences you will see between convection and conventional baking: Convection-baked items will rise faster, brown faster and tend to retain more moisture.

Keeping this in mind, there are certain guidelines that should be followed for consistently successful convection-baked products. These guidelines can also be used for converting your favorite recipes to convection recipes.

BAKING GUIDELINES

● **Decrease Temperature by 25 to 50 Degrees.** Because convection heat is more efficient than radiant (conventional) heat, decreasing the temperature is necessary in order to give a food a golden-brown exterior while cooking it all the way through. Manufacturer care-and-use booklets vary on their recommendations to reduce heat. Be sure to read your oven's care-and-use booklet. As a general rule, reducing temperature by 25 to 50 degrees is sufficient for most baked products. If you find a baked item sufficiently brown on the outside but underdone in the center, lower temperature an additional 25 degrees and increase baking time.

● **Reduce Baking Time.** When baking a new recipe in your convection oven, reduce temperature as recommended above and set timer for one-third less time than the recipe states. Test for doneness when the timer goes off. Continue baking if necessary. Usually foods will bake in one-fourth to one-third less time.

● **Use Metal Bakeware for Best Results.** Glass and flameproof ceramic baking pans may be used but may not result in reduced baking times. Aluminum, heavy-duty aluminum foil, black steel, cast iron and enameled cast iron can all be used with some time savings. Aluminum and heavy aluminum foil give the fastest cooking times. Remember that shiny metals will result in golden, tender products while black steel or black-coated bakeware will give browner, crustier products. Custards, such as the Individual Crème Caramels on page 50, and other egg-based foods that need gentle heating should be baked as they traditionally are in ceramic or glass bakeware. In such dishes, time is not as important as the gentleness of heating. See individual recipes for specific recommended bakeware.

● **Bake Several Small Items at a Time Rather Than One Large Item.** This is especially true with very rich moist batters and doughs. For fast, even baking, bake two or three small loaves of bread rather than one large one; bake individual brioches (page 29), rather than one large brioche. The reason is simple: The quick browning action of convection heat may cook the exterior of a large, thick item before the center is done. Large, high items, such as cheesecake or angel food cake, may be baked if the temperature is reduced and baking time increased.

● **Whenever Possible Use a Baking Sheet with No Sides.** This allows the circulating heat to surround items and brown evenly. If you do not have a baking sheet to fit the oven, turn over and use the bottom of a baking pan or jelly roll pan that does fit the oven.

● **Position Rack in Oven So Item Is Centered.** When two racks are used, position them so that both top and bottom foods are surrounded with at least one inch of air space.

● **Check the Temperature of Your Oven with an Oven Thermometer.** Periodically check the temperature of your oven with an accurate oven thermometer. If you find a discrepancy between the oven temperature setting and the actual oven temperature, adjust the temperature dial accordingly. If the discrepancy is more more than 25 degrees, contact your dealer or manufacturer.

● **Do Not Trust Your Eyes Alone to Determine When Foods Are Done.** While browning does indicate doneness, it isn't the only test. Because convection-baked items retain moisture, they are sometimes done when they don't *look* done. For example, a cake may look as if it is still gooey in the center but testing with a pick will show it is fully baked. Test items five to 10 minutes before the baking time is up. Test muffins, biscuits, cakes and soufflés with a wooden pick or metal cake tester. Test breads with a pick or by tapping; a hollow sound indicates doneness. Test cookies by removing one and breaking it open.

BAKING CONVENIENCE FOODS

Convection ovens handle convenience foods beautifully and in less time than the already speedy items usually take. For both packaged convenience foods such as cake, roll and cookie mixes, and frozen convenience foods such as TV dinners, frozen entrées and yeast bread dough, follow this routine: Reduce temperature by 25 degrees, bake according to package directions, reducing time by one fourth to one third. Note the actual cooking time for future reference. For maximum time savings when baking frozen convenience foods, bake at the recommended temperature and reduce time by one third, checking for doneness before continuing. If this method proves too harsh for the product (resulting in bubbling over or drying out of foods), follow the reduced temperature plan above.

QUICK AND YEAST ROLLS AND BREADS

RICH APPLE MUFFINS

A special muffin for company brunches.

Makes 12
1-3/4 cups unbleached all-purpose flour
1/2 cup sugar
3/4 teaspoon cream of tartar
1/2 teaspoon baking soda
1/2 teaspoon salt
1/4 teaspoon ground cinnamon
1 large egg
1/4 cup vegetable oil
1/2 cup whipping cream
1 cup diced peeled apple
2 teaspoons sugar
1/8 teaspoon ground cinnamon

Bakeware: 2 aluminum or heavy-duty aluminum foil 6-muffin tins

Preheat convection oven to 400°F. Sift together first 6 ingredients. In separate bowl, beat together egg, vegetable oil and whipping cream. Add to flour mixture and stir until just blended. Stir in diced apples. Batter will be thick. Spoon batter into greased muffin tins. Mix together 2 teaspoons sugar and 1/8 teaspoon cinnamon; sprinkle over batter. Bake in preheated oven for 12 to 15 minutes or until pick inserted in center of muffin comes out clean. Serve warm.

Standard oven: Preheat oven to 425°F; bake 15 to 16 minutes.

FRESH FRUIT SHORTCAKES

Fancy enough for guests, simple enough to serve any day.

Serves 6

SHORTCAKE BISCUITS
1-1/2 cups unbleached all-purpose flour
2-1/4 teaspoons baking powder
1/4 teaspoon salt
3 tablespoons sugar
6 tablespoons butter or margarine, softened
1 egg
3 tablespoons half-and-half

FILLING
3 cups sliced strawberries or peaches
2 tablespoons sugar
1 cup whipping cream

Bakeware: 1 aluminum or black steel baking sheet to fit oven

Preheat convection oven to 400°F. Stir together flour, baking powder, salt and 3 tablespoons sugar in mixing bowl. Cut in softened butter until mixture resembles cornmeal. Beat egg with half-and-half until well blended and stir into flour mixture until dough forms ball. If dough is sticky, add flour 1 teaspoon at a time until dough is easy to handle. If dough is too dry, add half-and-half in same manner. Refrigerate dough 15 minutes for easy handling. Roll out on lightly floured pastry board to 1/2-inch thickness. Cut 6 biscuits with floured 3-inch round biscuit cutter and place on greased baking sheet, leaving at least 1 inch of space between biscuits. Bake in preheated oven 8 to 10 minutes or until golden brown. While biscuits are cooling, toss sliced fruit with 2 tablespoons sugar and let stand to draw out juices. Beat whipping cream until stiff. To serve, split biscuits, fill with fruit and whipped cream and top with more fruit and whipped cream.

Standard oven: Preheat to 425°F; bake 10 to 12 minutes.

CELERY RYE BUNS

Make round rolls for hamburger buns or oval rolls for the bread basket.

Makes 12 large rolls
1 cup chopped celery
1 cup warm water (105° to 115°F)
1 tablespoon light molasses
1 package active dry yeast
Pinch of sugar
1 cup rye flour
1 tablespoon vegetable oil
1 teaspoon celery salt
1/2 teaspoon Seasoned Salt, page 138
2 to 2-1/2 cups unbleached all-purpose flour
1 egg white, slightly beaten
Celery seeds or poppy seeds

Bakeware: 2 aluminum baking sheets

Place celery and warm water in blender or food processor; process until liquified. Stir molasses into celery mixture in large mixing bowl. Add yeast and pinch of sugar and stir. Let stand in warm place until bubbly, about 5 minutes. Stir rye flour, oil and salts into yeast mixture. Beat until smooth. Stir in enough all-purpose flour to make a stiff dough. Turn dough out onto lightly floured pastry board. Knead until smooth and elastic, about 10 minutes. Place in clean oiled bowl, turn dough over, cover and let rise in warm place until doubled, about 1 hour.

To shape buns, punch down dough and divide in half. Cut each half into 6 pieces. Shape each piece into a ball or oval and place on greased baking sheet. Flatten slightly. Cover with towel and let rise in warm place until almost doubled in size, about 45 minutes. Preheat convection oven to 325°F. Brush each bun with egg white; sprinkle with celery seeds. Bake in preheated oven until golden brown and a pick inserted in center comes out clean, about 20 minutes.

Standard oven: Preheat to 375°F; bake about 20 minutes.

STICKY SNAIL ROLLS (Schnecken) ☆

A gooey treat that can be baked ahead, frozen and then reheated.

Makes 18
1/2 recipe No-knead White Bread and Roll
   Yeast Dough, page 31, or 1 package
   (13-3/4 ounces) hot roll mix
6 tablespoons melted butter
6 tablespoons warmed honey
3/4 cup brown sugar
6 tablespoons chopped pecans or walnuts

FILLING
2 tablespoons melted butter
1/2 teaspoon ground cinnamon
2 teaspoons grated lemon rind (yellow
   portion only)
2 tablespoons brown sugar
2 tablespoons chopped pecans or walnuts
2 tablespoons raisins

Bakeware: 3 aluminum or heavy-duty aluminum foil 6-muffin tins

Preheat convection oven to 325°F. Prepare 1/2 recipe No-knead White Bread and Roll Yeast Dough or hot roll mix according to package directions, up to point of shaping. While dough is rising, prepare muffin tins as follows: Pour 1 teaspoon melted butter, 1 teaspoon warmed honey, 2 teaspoons brown sugar and 1 teaspoon chopped nuts into each muffin cup. Divide dough in half. Roll each half into a square $8 \times 8 \times 1/4$ inch. Brush each square with 1 tablespoon melted butter and sprinkle with 1/4 teaspoon cinnamon, 1 teaspoon grated lemon rind, 1 tablespoon brown sugar, 1 tablespoon raisins. With a pizza cutter or sharp knife, cut each square into 9 equal strips. Roll up each strip pinwheel fashion and place in prepared muffin cup, cut side down. Let rise in warm place until double, about 30 minutes. Bake in preheated oven 15 to 20 minutes. Remove from oven, cool 2 minutes and invert muffin tin over cooling rack. Serve warm.

Standard oven: Preheat to 350°F; bake 20 minutes.

Note: To reheat cool rolls, wrap in aluminum foil, heat in 300°F convection oven for 10 minutes. To reheat frozen rolls, wrap in foil and heat in 300°F convection oven for 15 minutes.

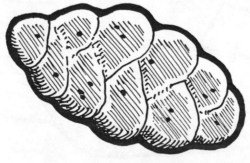

INDIVIDUAL CHOCOLATE CHIP BRIOCHES ☆

These freeze beautifully, so bake them ahead, freeze the whole batch and reheat when you want a special treat. Great for that special brunch, breakfast or coffee hour.

Makes 16
1 package active dry yeast
Pinch sugar
1/3 cup warm water (105° to 115°F)
6 ounces (1-1/2 sticks) unsalted butter or margarine, at room temperature
4 teaspoons sugar
4 large eggs, at room temperature
1 teaspoon salt
3 to 3-1/2 cups unbleached all-purpose flour
1/2 cup semisweet chocolate chips*
6 tablespoons unsalted butter, melted and cooled to room temperature
1 egg yolk
3 tablespoons milk
About 3 tablespoons sliced almonds
About 3 tablespoons sugar

Bakeware: Sixteen 3-inch heavy-duty aluminum foil fluted molds; 1 aluminum baking sheet to fit oven.

Stir yeast and pinch of sugar into warm water; set aside until bubbly, about 10 minutes. Beat butter in large bowl of electric mixer until light. Beat in sugar gradually. Beat in eggs, salt and 1 cup of the flour. Stir in yeast mixture; scrape down sides of bowl. Add another cup of flour and beat about 2 minutes. Beat in third cup of flour gradually. Stir in chocolate chips. Attach dough hook to mixer and knead dough about 5 minutes, adding remaining 1/2 cup flour if needed to make smooth, satiny dough. (Or turn out dough onto floured pastry board and knead by hand 5 minutes or until smooth.) Place dough in buttered bowl; turn buttered side up. Cover with plastic wrap and let rise in warm place until doubled, about 1-1/2 hours. Punch down dough with lightly floured hands, cover and refrigerate at least 6 hours or up to 24 hours.

To form brioches, preheat convection oven to 400°F (350°F for top-fan ovens). Brush fluted molds with cooled melted butter. Turn dough out onto lightly floured pastry board. Knead gently 1 to 2 minutes. Divide dough in half; wrap and refrigerate one half. Cut remaining half into 8 equal pieces. Shape each piece into a ball, drawing any seams to bottom of ball. Place in buttered molds and let rise in warm place until tripled, about 1 hour. Repeat with second half of dough. Mix together egg yolk and milk for glaze, brush top of each brioche with glaze and sprinkle with almonds and sugar. Bake in preheated oven 10 to 15 minutes or until brioche is golden brown and hollow-sounding when tapped. Unmold and serve warm with butter, if desired. Or, cool completely, wrap in heavy-duty aluminum foil and freeze.

Standard oven: Preheat to 425°F; bake about 20 minutes.

Note: To reheat frozen brioches, bake frozen brioches in aluminum foil in preheated 300°F convection oven (350°F standard oven) for 15 to 20 minutes.

*Be sure to use real chocolate, not imitation.

APRICOT NUT BREAD

A moist quick bread chock full of brandy-laced apricots and raisins. If you don't want the brandy flavoring, substitute additional orange juice.

Makes two 7-1/2 × 3-3/4-inch loaves
1 cup orange juice
1/2 cup apricot brandy
1 cup diced dried apricots
1/2 cup golden raisins
1 egg, lightly beaten
1 cup firmly packed brown sugar
3 tablespoons vegetable oil
1 tablespoon grated orange peel (orange portion only)
2-1/2 cups unbleached all-purpose flour
1 teaspoon salt
2 teaspoons baking powder
1/2 teaspoon baking soda
1 cup chopped walnuts

Bakeware: Two 7-1/2 × 3-3/4 × 2-inch aluminum or heavy-duty aluminum foil loaf pans

Preheat convection oven to 300°F. Bring orange juice and brandy to a simmer. Remove from heat, add apricots and raisins and let stand 1/2 hour. Beat together egg, brown sugar, vegetable oil and orange rind. Stir in apricot mixture. Stir together flour, salt, baking powder and soda. Add to apricot mixture and beat well. Stir in walnuts. Pour into greased loaf pans. Bake in preheated oven about 25 minutes or until pick inserted in center comes out clean. Cool 15 minutes and remove from pans.

Standard oven: Preheat to 325°F; bake 30 to 35 minutes.

CRUNCHY BREADSTICKS

The next time you serve pasta, surprise the family with homemade breadsticks.

Makes 8
1/3 recipe Pizza Dough, page 134
Olive oil
Kosher salt or Seasoned Salt, page 138

Bakeware: 1 aluminum or black steel baking sheet to fit oven

Preheat convection oven to 425°F. Punch down dough and knead briefly on lightly floured pastry board. Cut dough into 8 equal pieces. With palms of hands, roll each piece into long rope 1/2 to 3/4 inch in diameter. Brush baking sheet lightly with olive oil and sprinkle generously with kosher or seasoned salt. Place ropes on baking sheet, leaving 1 inch of space between ropes. Brush with olive oil and sprinkle with kosher or seasoned salt. Bake in preheated oven 12 to 15 minutes or until breadsticks are crisp and golden brown. Cool on wire racks. For even crispier breadsticks, leave at room temperature overnight.

Standard oven: Preheat to 425°F; bake about 15 minutes.

NO-KNEAD WHITE BREAD AND ROLL YEAST DOUGH

This refrigerator dough can be made one day and baked the next in a variety of shapes.

Makes 2 large loaves,
4 small loaves or 48 crescent rolls
2 packages active dry yeast
2 cups warm water (105°115°F)
1/2 cup sugar
1/2 cup soft butter or margarine
2 teaspoons salt
1 large egg
1 cup instant nonfat dry milk
6-1/2 to 7 cups unbleached all-purpose flour
Melted butter or margarine

Bakeware: Two 8-1/2 × 4-1/2 × 2-1/2-inch or four 7-1/2 × 3-1/2 × 2-1/4-inch metal loaf pans or 2 aluminum baking sheets to fit oven

Stir yeast into warm water in large mixer bowl. Add sugar, butter, salt, egg, dry milk and about 3 cups of the flour and beat at low speed until ingredients are moistened. Beat at medium speed until mixture is smooth, about 1 minute. Gradually stir in enough of the remaining flour to make dough easy to handle. It should be soft but not sticky. Brush clean bowl with melted butter, place dough in bowl and turn greased side up. Cover loosely with plastic wrap and refrigerate at least 8 hours or overnight. Punch down and knead dough very briefly on lightly floured pastry board. Shape and bake loaves or rolls as follows:

To make large loaves: Roll out one half of the dough into an 11 × 8-inch rectangle on lightly floured pastry board. Beginning at 8-inch edge, roll up dough to form loaf and place in greased 8-1/2 × 4-1/2 × 2-1/2-inch loaf pan seam side down. Brush with melted butter and let rise in warm place until double, 1 to 1-1/2 hours. Preheat convection oven to 350°F. Brush loaves with melted butter, slash top if desired and bake in preheated oven 20 to 25 minutes or until pick inserted in center comes out clean. Cool in pan 10 minutes and remove from pan.

To make small loaves: Roll out one fourth of the dough into a 10 × 7-inch rectangle on a lightly floured pastry board. Beginning at 7-inch edge, roll up dough to form loaf and place in greased 7-1/2 × 3-1/2 × 2-1/4-inch loaf pan seam side down. Brush with melted butter and let rise in warm place until double, about 1 hour. Preheat convection oven to 350°F. Brush loaves with melted butter, slash tops if desired and bake in preheated oven 20 to 25 minutes or until pick inserted in center comes out clean. Cool in pan 10 minutes and remove from pan.

To make crescent rolls: Roll out one fourth of the dough into an 11-inch circle on lightly floured pastry board. Brush with melted butter and cut into 12 wedges with pastry or pizza cutter. Roll up wedges beginning at wide end. Turn ends in to form crescent and place on greased baking sheets point side down, leaving 2 inches of space between crescents. Repeat with remaining dough. Brush crescents with melted butter and let rise in warm place until double, about 1 hour. Preheat convection oven to 350°F. Brush crescents with melted butter and bake in preheated oven 8 to 10 minutes or until crescents are golden brown.

Standard oven: Preheat to 375°F; bake large loaves 25 to 35 minutes, small loaves 20 to 25 minutes and crescent rolls 12 to 15 minutes.

WHOLE-WHEAT RAISIN BREAD

This batter bread is delicious spread with cream cheese and makes lovely toast.

Makes 1 loaf
1 package active dry yeast
1/4 cup warm water (105° to 115°F)
1 cup milk
2 tablespoons packed brown sugar
2 tablespoons butter or margarine
1-1/2 teaspoons salt
1 egg, beaten
1/2 cup raisins
1-1/2 cups unbleached all-purpose flour
1-1/2 cups stone-ground whole-wheat flour

Bakeware: 1 aluminum or heavy-duty aluminum foil loaf pan

Preheat convection oven to 325°F. Dissolve yeast in 1/4 cup warm water in large mixing bowl. Stir together milk, brown sugar, butter and salt in saucepan over low heat until butter is melted. Cool to lukewarm. Stir into yeast mixture; stir in egg and raisins. Gradually stir in flours and mix well. If batter appears too sticky, stir in an additional 2 tablespoons all-purpose flour. Cover bowl with towel and let rise in warm place until doubled in size, 45 to 60 minutes. Stir down dough and beat 1 minute. Pat dough into greased loaf pan. Cover with a sheet of greased waxed paper and let rise in warm place until dough reaches top of pan, about 45 minutes. Bake in center of preheated oven 30 to 40 minutes or until loaf is brown and wooden pick inserted in center comes out clean. Remove from oven and let cool in pan 10 minutes. Remove from pan. Cool completely.

Standard oven: Preheat to 375°F; bake 40 to 45 minutes.

GRANDMA'S HOUSKA (Braided Raisin Bread)

A recipe from my grandmother's kitchen that is a traditional favorite in Czech homes at Christmas time but is good all year round. If your oven cavity is large enough to hold a large baking sheet, you can double this recipe and bake the houskas on one rack side by side.

Makes 1 loaf
1/4 cup milk
1 package active dry yeast
1/2 teaspoon sugar
6 tablespoons milk
4 tablespoons (1/2 stick) unsalted butter or margarine, cut into chunks
2 eggs
1/4 cup sugar
1 tablespoon grated lemon rind (yellow portion only)
1/2 teaspoon salt
About 2-1/2 cups unbleached all-purpose flour
1/4 cup slivered blanched almonds
1/2 cup golden raisins, soaked in warm water to plump, drained
Additional flour

GLAZE
1 egg yolk
1 tablespoon milk

Bakeware: 1 aluminum baking sheet to fit oven

Preheat convection oven to 325°F. Heat 1/4 cup milk to lukewarm, pour into measuring cup and add dry yeast and 1/2 teaspoon sugar. Stir and set in a warm place until mixture bubbles up and doubles in volume, about 5 minutes.

Heat 6 tablespoons milk to just below boiling, add butter, stir to melt and let cool to lukewarm. In large mixing bowl, beat eggs and add 1/4 cup sugar, lemon rind, salt and yeast mixture in that order. Stir to mix well. Gradually stir in 2-1/2 cups flour or more to make a soft but not sticky dough. Stir in slivered almonds and raisins. Turn out onto lightly floured pastry board. Knead 3 to 5 minutes or until smooth and slightly elastic. Place in buttered bowl, turn buttered side up, cover loosely with clean towel and let rise in warm place until dough doubles in bulk, about 45 minutes. Punch down and knead on pastry board 2 to 3 minutes. Return to bowl and let rise again until double, about 30 minutes.

Punch dough down and divide into 3 equal pieces. Roll each piece into a rope about 15 inches long, making rope slightly thicker in the center than on the ends. Pinch the 3 ropes together at one end. Braid ropes, pinch remaining ends together and tuck ends under braid. Cover baking sheet with piece of cooking parchment and place braided loaf on baking sheet. Let rise in warm place about 30 minutes. If any raisins pop through surface of dough, gently push them into dough to prevent scorching while baking. Mix egg yolk and 1 tablespoon milk together for glaze. Brush entire surface of braided loaf with glaze. Center loaf in preheated oven and bake 20 to 25 minutes or until houska is brown and loaf sounds hollow when tapped. If houska begins to brown too quickly, turn temperature down to 300°F and increase baking time. Cool loaf, slice and serve as is or with butter and jam. Delicious as toast, too.

Standard oven: Preheat to 350°F; bake 25 to 30 minutes.

FINNISH RYE BREAD

An easy yet exceptionally light bread. It rises only once and then gets a boost in the oven from the bread flour. Bread flour is higher in gluten than all-purpose flour; this gluten gives breads extra rise. Bread flour is available in many supermarkets. If unavailable, unbleached all-purpose flour may be substituted.

Makes 1 loaf
1 package active dry yeast
Pinch of sugar
1 tablespoon light or dark molasses
1/4 cup warm water (105° to 115°F)
2/3 cup water
1 tablespoon soft butter or margarine
2 teaspoons fennel seeds
1 teaspoon salt
3/4 cup rye flour
About 1-3/4 cups bread flour

Bakeware: 1 aluminum baking sheet to fit oven

Stir yeast, sugar and molasses into 1/4 cup warm water in large mixing bowl. Let stand until bubbly, about 10 minutes. Add 2/3 cup water, butter, fennel seeds and salt to yeast mixture. Stir in rye flour and enough bread flour to make a stiff dough. Turn out onto floured pastry board and knead until smooth and elastic, about 10 minutes. Shape into a smooth ball and place on greased baking sheet. Flatten ball slightly. Cover with towel and let rise in warm place until doubled in size, about 30 to 45 minutes. Preheat convection oven to 325°F. Bake loaf in preheated oven 25 to 30 minutes or until loaf is brown and sounds hollow when tapped.

Standard oven: Preheat to 375°F; bake 25 to 30 minutes.

Note: This bread can be made in a food processor as follows: With steel blade in place, add flours, butter and fennel seeds to processor bowl and process 5 seconds. Add yeast mixture and process 5 seconds. With processor on, slowly add 2/3 cup water through feed tube and continue to process until dough leaves sides of bowl. If dough does not form ball, add small amount of water. Shape and bake as above.

APPETIZERS AND SAVORY PIES

CHINESE BARBECUED PORK

A spicy appetizer with an authentic Chinese flavor derived from brown bean sauce and hot pepper powder.

Serves 6 to 8 as appetizer
2 pounds boneless pork shoulder
2 teaspoons salt
1/2 cup sugar
1/2 teaspoon five-spice powder*

MARINADE
1/3 cup American barbecue sauce
2/3 cup catsup
3 tablespoons dark soy sauce*
4 teaspoons brown bean sauce*
3/4 teaspoon Chinese hot pepper powder* or cayenne pepper
2 garlic cloves, crushed

Shredded lettuce

Bakeware: One 7 × 11 × 1-1/2-inch metal baking pan

Cut pork shoulder lengthwise into 2 or 3 strips. Each strip should be about 2 inches across. Trim away excess fat. Place strips in baking pan. Stir together salt, sugar and five-spice powder; pour over pork in pan. Let stand 1-1/2 to 2 hours (no longer than 2 hours).

Preheat convection oven to 325°F. Stir together marinade ingredients; pour over pork. Stir gently to coat all pieces with marinade. Bake in preheated oven 30 minutes. Turn over pork pieces and bake another 30 minutes. If desired, turn oven to 400°F for last 2 to 3 minutes to brown meat. Remove pork to cutting board and let rest 10 minutes. Skim fat from pan juices, pour juices into saucepan and bring to boil. Slice pork 1/4 inch thick and arrange on platter over shredded lettuce. Spoon just enough hot juices over pork to glaze. Use remaining juices as dipping sauce, if desired. Serve warm or at room temperature.

Standard oven: Preheat to 350°F; bake 40 minutes, then 35 minutes.

*Available at Chinese food markets or in Chinese sections of some supermarkets.

OYSTERS BAKED WITH GARLIC O

Fresh oysters cooked to a delicate turn to rival any restaurant's version.

Serves 4 as an appetizer
Soft butter or margarine
3 tablespoons unsalted butter or margarine
1 cup soft bread crumbs made from day-old Italian or French bread
2 garlic cloves, minced
1 tablespoon minced parsley
1 tablespoon grated Parmesan cheese
1 dozen shucked fresh oysters
1 tablespoon unsalted butter or margarine, cut into bits
4 lemon wedges
24 small parsley sprigs

Bakeware: 4 baking shells or four 1/2-cup ceramic ramekins or custard cups

Preheat convection oven to 400°F. Grease shells generously with soft butter. Melt 3 tablespoons butter in a medium skillet until foam subsides. Add the bread crumbs and garlic and toss over medium heat for 2 or 3 minutes or until crumbs are slightly crisp and golden brown. Remove from heat and stir in parsley. Spread about 2 tablespoons crumb mixture in each shell and mix remaining crumbs with the grated Parmesan cheese. Place three oysters in each shell in a single layer and top with the cheese-crumb mixture. Dot the tops with the butter bits. Place shells on oven rack and slide into center of preheated oven. Bake 8 to 10 minutes or until crumbs are brown and oysters are slightly springy to the touch. Place each shell on an appetizer plate, garnish with lemon wedge and parsley sprig and serve immediately.

Standard oven: Preheat to 425°F; bake in upper half of oven about 12 minutes.

CRABMEAT STRUDEL

Crispy fillo leaves surround a creamy crabmeat filling. Look for fillo leaves in the freezer section of your supermarket.

Makes 24 appetizer servings

1/4 pound (1 stick) unsalted butter or
    margarine
1/2 cup chopped shallots or onion
1/4 cup chopped celery
 1 cup dry white vermouth
2 cans (6 ounces each) crabmeat, drained
    and flaked
1 package (4 ounces) cream cheese, cubed
1/4 cup minced parsley
4 egg yolks, lightly beaten
1 teaspoon salt
1/2 teaspoon freshly ground white pepper
8 frozen fillo leaves, thawed according to
    package directions
6 tablespoons melted butter or margarine
1 egg, beaten
Parsley sprigs
Lemon wedges

Bakeware: One 15-1/2 × 10-1/2 × 1-inch alum inum jelly roll pan or 2 smaller jelly roll pans to fit oven

Melt 1/4 pound butter in 10-inch skillet, add shallots and celery and cook over medium heat until tender and golden, 3 to 5 minutes. Add the vermouth, bring to a boil and boil until liquid is reduced by half, about 5 minutes. Remove from heat and stir in crabmeat, cream cheese, parsley, egg yolks, salt and pepper until cream cheese melts. Cool to handling temperature.

Preheat convection oven to 325°F. On flat work surface, place 1 fillo leaf on a sheet of waxed paper and brush all over with melted butter. Place a second leaf on top of the first one and brush with melted butter. Repeat until 4 fillo leaves are stacked up. Spoon one half of the crabmeat mixture lengthwise onto fillo leaves 2 inches from 1 long edge. To begin rolling, lift edge of paper so fillo comes up over filling, and continue to roll jelly roll fashion. Cylinder should be about 2 inches in diameter. Brush jelly roll pan with melted butter and place strudel on pan seam side down. Repeat stacking and rolling with remaining fillo leaves and filling.

Place second strudel on jelly roll pan leaving at least 2 inches of space between strudels. (If using 2 jelly roll pans, make 4 half-size strudels by cutting fillo leaf stack in half with sharp knife or pastry cutter before filling and rolling. Place 2 strudels on each pan.) Brush top of each strudel with melted butter, then with beaten egg. Bake in center of preheated oven 10 to 12 minutes, then increase temperature to 400°F and bake another 5 to 10 minutes or until strudels are brown and crisp. To serve, cut each strudel crosswise into 12 pieces, arrange on platter and garnish with parsley sprigs and lemon wedges. (If baking 4 small strudels, cut each into 6 pieces.) To make strudels ahead, bake and cool, wrap in plastic and aluminum foil and freeze for up to 1 week. To heat, place on jelly roll pan and bake in center of preheated 325°F oven 10 to 15 minutes or until hot throughout.

Standard oven: Preheat to 350°F; bake about 15 minutes, increase temperature to 450°F and bake another 5 to 10 minutes.

SOY CHICKEN WINGS ☆

An Oriental appetizer that's especially attractive served on a bed of shredded lettuce.

Makes 24
24 chicken wings
1 cup soy sauce
3/4 cup finely chopped green onions
1/3 cup sugar
1 teaspoon Oriental sesame oil
2 teaspoons vegetable oil
2 garlic cloves, crushed
1 tablespoon minced ginger root

Bakeware: Two 8 × 12-inch aluminum or heavy-duty aluminum foil shallow baking pans or any size to fit oven

Preheat convection oven to 325°F. Chop off chicken wing tips and discard. Bend back wing at joint to disjoint. Pat wings dry with paper toweling. Combine remaining ingredients in large bowl. Add chicken wings and marinate 30 minutes, mixing wings once to make sure they are coated. Arrange wings in single layer in baking pans. Bake uncovered in preheated oven 15 minutes. Turn wings, baste with marinade and bake another 15 minutes. Serve warm or at room temperature.

Standard oven: Preheat to 350°F; bake 20 minutes per side.

THIS 'N THAT PASTRIES

This appetizer or snack can be put together anytime you have a little bit of this and a little bit of that leftover in the refrigerator.

Leftover French Pastry Dough, page 136, or
    Basic Pie Dough, page 135
2 tablespoons grated Parmesan cheese
1 tablespoon finely chopped nuts
Pinch salt
Freshly ground pepper
2 teaspoons finely chopped green pimiento-stuffed olives

Bakeware: 1 or 2 aluminum baking sheets

Preheat convection oven to 375°F. On lightly floured pastry board, roll out leftover pastry dough to 1/8-inch thickness. Cut into circles with a 3-inch pastry cutter or edge of a glass dipped in flour. Combine remaining ingredients. Place about 1 teaspoon filling in center of each circle, wet half of edge with cold water, fold circle in half and press edge closed. Seal by pressing with tines of a fork dipped in flour. Place on pastry sheet, leaving 1-1/2 inches between pastries. Bake in preheated oven for 12 to 15 minutes or until golden brown.

Standard oven: Preheat oven to 400°F; bake about 15 minutes.

CHEDDAR CHEESE TARTLETS ☆

A very special hors d'oeuvre that is definitely party fare.

Makes about 24
1/2 recipe French Pastry Dough, page 136
3/4 cup diced sharp Cheddar cheese
  (1/4-inch dice)
1/2 cup minced shallots or onions

FILLING
1 cup Crème Fraîche, page 132, or whipping
  cream
1 cup shredded sharp Cheddar cheese
1/2 teaspoon salt
1/8 teaspoon (or more) cayenne pepper
2 eggs
3/4 cup grated Parmesan cheese

Bakeware: Twenty-four 2-1/2-inch round or diamond-shaped tartlet molds, 3/4 inch deep; 2 aluminum baking sheets to fit oven

Preheat convection oven to 375°F. To line tartlet molds, allow pastry dough to sit at room temperature for about 5 minutes, then roll out to a generous 1/8-inch thickness using small amount of flour to keep dough from sticking to work surface. Group tartlet molds on work surface, place rolled dough over molds and gently push dough into each mold, easing dough so it does not tear. Roll rolling pin over top of molds to cut dough. Gather up dough scraps and refrigerate. Push dough into bottom of each mold to fill corners. With thumb, push dough up over top edge of mold slightly all around. Place tartlets on baking sheets, leaving space around each one. Push 5 to 6 Cheddar cheese dice into bottom of each tartlet so cheese sticks in dough. Spoon about 1/2 teaspoon minced shallot into each tartlet, pushing down gently with back of spoon. Refrigerate while making filling.

To make filling, heat crème fraîche, shredded Cheddar cheese and salt and pepper in small saucepan over medium low heat until cheese melts. Remove from heat and cool 5 minutes. Beat eggs in mixing bowl to blend. Slowly add cheese mixture, beating eggs constantly. (Tartlets can be completed to this point several hours ahead of time. Refrigerate filling and molds separately until ready to bake.) Spoon filling into prepared molds so each is three-fourths full. Sprinkle about 1 teaspoon Parmesan over filling in each mold. Bake in preheated oven on 1 or 2 racks for 15 to 16 minutes or until crust is brown and filling is brown and puffed. Remove from oven and allow to cool 5 minutes. Remove from molds and serve warm or at room temperature.

Standard oven: Preheat to 400°F; bake about 16 minutes.

Note: To reheat tartlets, place directly on convection oven rack and heat to 300°F for 5 to 10 minutes.

VARIATION To add a tomatoey tang, spoon 1 teaspoon Pizza Sauce, page 133, onto center of filling before sprinkling with Parmesan.

PEPPERONI CHEESE APPETIZERS

A crunchy pastry filled with pepperoni and mozzarella and spiced with a variety of flavorings.

Makes about 45
1 recipe Pizza Dough, page 134
3-inch piece of pepperoni, cut into 1/8-inch slices
About 3 ounces mozzarella cheese, cut into 1/4 × 1/4 × 1-inch sticks
Oregano
Olive oil
Anchovy paste (optional)
Red pepper flakes (optional)
Capers, drained (optional)

Bakeware: 1 or more aluminum or black steel baking sheets to fit oven

Preheat convection oven to 400°F. Roll out pizza dough to 1/8-inch thickness on lightly floured surface. Dough will be elastic; begin by stretching it gently with your fingers. With a 3-inch biscuit cutter, cut dough into rounds. Gather up scraps, roll out and cut as before. Cut pepperoni slices in half. Place 1 piece of pepperoni and 1 piece of mozzarella on each dough round. Sprinkle with a small pinch of oregano and 1 or 2 drops olive oil. Add a dab of anchovy paste, a few red pepper flakes or 2 capers to each round if desired. Brush one half of the edge of each round with water, fold rounds in half and press edge closed with tines of a fork. Brush baking sheet with olive oil and place pastries on baking sheet leaving at least 1 inch of space between pastries. Brush lightly with olive oil and bake in preheated oven 10 to 12 minutes or until golden brown. Serve warm or at room temperature as finger food.

Standard oven: Preheat to 425°F; bake 12 to 15 minutes.

NEOPOLITAN THIN-CRUST PIZZA

A delicate crust makes this pizza something special.

Makes one 9 × 12-inch pizza
1/3 recipe Pizza Dough, page 134
Flour
1 teaspoon cornmeal
1/2 recipe Pizza Sauce, page 133
1 cup shredded mozzarella cheese
Thinly sliced green pepper, mushrooms or onion, and/or small pieces of Italian sausage (out of casing) or 1/8-inch-thick slices of pepperoni
1 tablespoon grated Parmesan cheese
1 to 2 teaspoons olive oil (use less on sausage pizza)

Bakeware: 1 aluminum or black steel baking sheet to fit oven

Preheat convection oven to 450°F. Punch down and knead briefly on lightly floured pastry board. Pick up and stretch in circular motion, return to board and flatten into rectangle with hand. Roll out to 9 × 12-inch rectangle or any size to fit oven. Sprinkle cornmeal on baking sheet. Transfer rolled dough to baking sheet and crimp edge all around between thumb and forefinger to form rim. Bake in center of preheated oven 8 to 10 minutes or until dough is set and pale brown. If bubbles form, deflate with a fork. Remove from oven and spread pizza sauce over dough with back of spoon. Sprinkle on mozzarella cheese and top with thinly sliced vegetables and/or pieces of sausage or pepperoni as desired. Sprinkle Parmesan over top and drizzle with olive oil. Return to low rack in preheated oven and bake 8 to 10 minutes or until crust is golden brown and filling is bubbling.

Standard oven: Preheat to 500°F; assemble pizza without prebaking crust and bake 10 to 12 minutes.

EXTRA-CHEESY QUICHE

A rich quiche that's perfect as a first course or for lunch with a salad.

Serves 6 as a first course, 4 for lunch
1/2 recipe French Pastry Dough, page 136
1/2 cup diced Gruyère cheese (1/4-inch dice)
2 large eggs
1 cup whipping cream
1/2 teaspoon salt
Several grindings black pepper
Freshly grated nutmeg
1/2 cup grated Gruyère or combination of
  grated Gruyère and Parmesan

Bakeware: One 9-inch aluminum quiche pan with removable bottom, 1 inch deep

Preheat convection oven to 375°F. Roll out pastry dough to 1/8-inch thickness using small amount of flour to keep dough from sticking to work surface. Roll onto rolling pin and unroll over quiche pan. Ease dough into pan so it fits into corners. Roll rolling pin over top edge of pan to cut dough. Gather up scraps and refrigerate. (Scraps can be used for Cheddar Cheese Tartlets, page 39, or This 'n That Pastries, page 38.) Push dough into bottom of pan and with thumb push dough up above pan edge all around, pushing it out slightly so dough hooks over pan edge. Sprinkle diced Gruyère over bottom of filled pan and push dice into dough. Refrigerate or place in freezer while making filling.

In mixing bowl, beat together eggs and whipping cream. Add salt, pepper and nutmeg; taste and correct seasonings. Pour into prepared quiche pan. Sprinkle grated cheese over filling. Bake in center of preheated oven for 20 to 25 minutes or until crust is brown and filling is brown and crackled. Remove from oven, allow to cool 5 minutes and unmold by removing sides of pan. Serve warm or at room temperature.

Standard oven: Preheat oven to 400°F; place quiche pan on baking sheet, bake 20 to 25 minutes.

Note: Because cheese melts into dough, bottom crust of quiche may remain soft, even after completely baking.

MOLDED HAM AND LEEK QUICHE ☆

A crustless quiche is easy to make and beautiful to serve.

Serves 8 as a first course, 6 for lunch
About 1 tablespoon soft butter or margarine
About 3 tablespoons dry bread crumbs
3 large leeks
3 tablespoons butter or margarine
1 package (8 ounces) cream cheese, softened
1 cup sour cream
2 eggs
2 egg yolks
2 cups finely chopped ham (about 6 ounces)
1/2 teaspoon salt
Freshly ground pepper to taste
1/4 teaspoon Herbes de Provence, page 137
3 tablespoons minced parsley (leaves only)
1/4 cup Crème Fraîche, page 132, at room
  temperature (optional)
Paprika

Bakeware: One 9-inch round aluminum cake pan with non-stick surface; 1 rectangular 11-5/8 × 9-1/4-inch heavy-duty aluminum foil baking pan or any size to fit oven and accommodate cake pan (to be used as water bath)

Preheat convection oven to 325°F. Butter cake pan with soft butter and coat bottom and sides with bread crumbs. Place in freezer to set. Using only the white portion of the leeks, wash thoroughly, then cut lengthwise into fourths and crosswise into 1/4-inch pieces. Melt butter in 10-inch skillet, add leeks and cook over low heat, stirring often, until tender and glossy (but not brown), about 20 minutes. Make filling while leeks cook: Beat cream cheese in large mixing bowl until fluffy. Stir in sour cream. Beat eggs and yolks to blend and stir into cream cheese mixture. Add ham, salt, pepper, Herbes de Provence and 2 tablespoons of the minced parsley. Pour filling into prepared cake pan, set pan in rectangular baking pan and add boiling water to rectangular pan to come halfway up the side of cake pan. Bake in preheated oven 15 to 20 minutes or until sharp knife inserted in center comes out clean. To unmold, run small spatula around edge of quiche, set inverted platter over quiche, turn over and lift off cake pan. Immediately spread the crème fraîche over the quiche, sprinkle with remaining tablespoon of parsley and a little paprika for color. Cut into wedges to serve.

Standard oven: Preheat to 350°F; bake 20 to 25 minutes.

WHEAT AND PEANUT BUTTER WAFERS

Nutty snack wafers that may be served with butter or cream cheese.

Makes about 3 dozen
1/4 cup chunky peanut butter
2 tablespoons butter or margarine
3 tablespoons packed brown sugar
2 tablespoons granulated sugar
1/2 cup plus 2 tablespoons whole-wheat flour
1/2 cup plus 2 tablespoons unbleached
   all-purpose flour
1/2 teaspoon baking powder
1/2 teaspoon baking soda
1/4 teaspoon salt
1/4 cup milk
1 egg yolk

Bakeware: 1 or more aluminum or black steel baking sheets to fit oven

Beat together peanut butter, butter and sugars until light and fluffy. In separate bowls, stir together dry ingredients and milk and egg yolk. Add dry ingredients alternately with liquid to peanut butter mixture to form a dough. If mixture appears crumbly, add milk a teaspoonful at a time. Shape into ball, flatten into patty, wrap and refrigerate about 45 minutes. Preheat convection oven to 325°F. Divide dough in half; keep 1 half in refrigerator while working the other half. Roll each half to a 1/8-inch thickness on a lightly floured surface. With biscuit cutter, cut into 2-inch rounds. Place on ungreased baking sheets, leaving about 1 inch of space between rounds. Pierce surface of rounds with a fork and bake in preheated oven 8 to 12 minutes or until deep golden brown. If using 2 racks, bake bottom rack 3 to 5 minutes more.

Standard oven: Preheat to 375°F; bake 10 to 12 minutes.

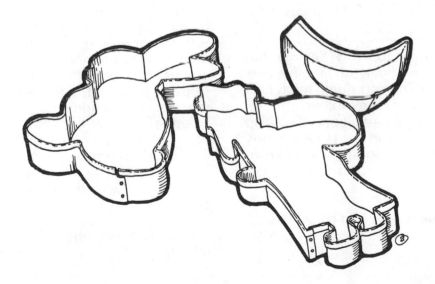

CONFECTIONS AND COOKIES

JAM CRUNCH BARS O

This treat goes together quickly and will be an instant hit.

Makes 16 bar cookies
1-1/2 cups sifted unbleached all-purpose flour
1/4 teaspoon salt
1 teaspoon baking powder
1-1/2 cups quick-cooking rolled oats
1 cup packed brown sugar
6 ounces (1-1/2 sticks) butter or margarine, cut into 1/2-inch dice
3/4 cup raspberry or apricot preserves

Bakeware: One 11 × 7 × 1-1/2-inch metal baking pan

Preheat convection oven to 350°F. Sift together flour, salt and baking powder. Stir in rolled oats and brown sugar. Cut in butter until mixture is crumbly. Pat two thirds of the mixture into the bottom of baking pan. Spread on preserves, top with remaining mixture and press very gently with fingers to smooth top slightly. Bake in preheated oven 25 to 30 minutes. Cool and cut into 16 bars.

Standard oven: Preheat to 375°F; bake 30 to 35 minutes.

SUGAR 'N SPICE ALMONDS

A sweet and crunchy confection for the buffet table.

Makes about 1 cup
1 egg white
1 tablespoon frozen orange juice concentrate, thawed
1 teaspoon grated orange rind (orange portion only)
1/2 cup confectioners' sugar
1/4 cup granulated sugar
1/8 teaspoon ground cinnamon
Dash of ground cloves
1/8 teaspoon salt
1 cup whole unblanched almonds

Bakeware: 1 aluminum or black steel baking sheet to fit oven

Preheat convection oven to 275°F. Beat egg white until foamy in small mixing bowl. Stir in orange juice concentrate and orange rind. In separate bowl, mix together all remaining ingredients except almonds. Stir 2 tablespoons almonds into egg white mixture, remove with slotted spoon, let drain well and toss in sugar mixture. Place almonds close together on greased baking sheet. Repeat with remaining almonds. Bake in preheated oven 20 to 25 minutes or until coating is crispy. Remove nuts from baking sheet, breaking apart, if necessary. Cool completely on waxed paper. Store in airtight container.

Standard oven: Preheat to 300°F; bake 25 to 30 minutes.

RASPBERRY MERINGUE KISSES

A light treat with a surprising chocolate center. Nice as an ice cream accompaniment.

Makes about 3 dozen
3 egg whites, at room temperature
1 teaspoon vinegar
1/8 teaspoon salt
1 package (3 ounces) raspberry gelatin
3/4 cup sugar
1 package (6 ounces) semisweet chocolate
   chips

Bakeware: 2 aluminum cookie sheets

Preheat convection oven to 250°F. Beat egg whites until foamy, add vinegar and salt and continue to beat until soft peaks form. Gradually beat in gelatin and sugar. Continue to beat until stiff, glossy peaks form. Fold in chocolate chips. Drop by heaping teaspoonfuls onto buttered cookie sheets. Bake in preheated oven for 30 minutes. Do not open oven door. Turn off oven and leave meringues in oven for an additional 20 minutes. Remove meringues from oven, cool and store in airtight container.

Standard oven: Preheat to 250°F; bake meringues 25 minutes, turn off oven and leave meringues in oven an additional 20 minutes.

CRACKLED CRISPY COOKIES O

A crunchy munchy for after-school milk time.

Makes about 3 dozen
1/4 pound (1 stick) unsalted butter or
   margarine, softened
1/2 cup packed brown sugar
1/2 cup granulated sugar
1 large egg, beaten
1 teaspoon vanilla extract
1 cup unbleached all-purpose flour
1/4 teaspoon ground cinnamon
Several gratings nutmeg
1/4 teaspoon salt
1/2 teaspoon baking soda
1/4 teaspoon baking powder
1 cup oatmeal
1 cup cornflakes
1/2 cup shredded coconut
1/2 cup chopped walnuts

Bakeware: 2 aluminum cookie sheets

Preheat convection oven to 350°F. Cream butter, add sugars and beat until fluffy. Beat in egg and vanilla. Sift together dry ingredients and gradually beat into butter mixture. Stir in oatmeal, cornflakes, coconut and nuts. Dough will be stiff. Form into small balls (about 1 heaping teaspoonful each) and place on greased cookie sheet 2 inches apart. Flatten slightly and bake in preheated oven 10 to 12 minutes or until cookies are crackled and golden. Remove to cooling rack.

Standard oven: Preheat to 350°F; bake 12 to 14 minutes.

HONEYED CHOCOLATE CHIP COOKIES

Chocolate chip cookies made with one of nature's purest ingredients—golden honey.

Makes about 5 dozen
1/4 pound (1 stick) butter or margarine, softened
1/2 cup honey
1 large egg
1 teaspoon vanilla extract
1-1/2 cups unbleached all-purpose flour
1/2 teaspoon baking soda
1/4 teaspoon baking powder
1/2 teaspoon salt
1/2 cup chopped walnuts or pecans
1 cup semisweet chocolate chips

Bakeware: 1 or more aluminum or black steel baking sheets to fit oven

Preheat convection oven to 325°F. Beat butter in large mixing bowl until fluffy. Add honey and beat until smooth. Beat in egg and vanilla. Stir together flour, baking soda, baking powder and salt; stir into honey mixture until well blended. Stir in walnuts and chocolate chips. Drop by rounded teaspoonfuls onto lightly greased baking sheets, leaving about 1 inch of space between cookies. Flatten each cookie slightly and bake in preheated oven 10 to 12 minutes to until golden brown. If using 2 racks, bake bottom rack 3 to 5 minutes more. Cool on baking sheets 2 to 3 minutes and remove to cooling rack.

Standard oven: Preheat to 350°F; bake cookies about 12 minutes.

DAINTY CHOCOLATE CRACKLERS

These cookies will rise during baking, then fall and crackle slightly. They should be crispy to the bite.

Makes about 5 dozen
1-1/2 cups sifted unbleached all-purpose flour
3/4 teaspoon baking soda
1/2 teaspoon salt
6 tablespoons butter or margarine
3/4 cup packed brown sugar
1 tablespoon water
1 package (6 ounces) semisweet chocolate chips
1 egg

Bakeware: 1 or more aluminum or black steel baking sheets to fit oven

Preheat convection oven to 325°F. Stir together flour, baking soda and salt; set aside. Begin to melt butter in heavy saucepan. Add brown sugar and stir over low heat until all butter is melted. Remove from heat and stir in water. Add chocolate chips and stir until melted. Beat in egg. Gradually stir in dry ingredients until mixture is smooth. Drop by level teaspoonfuls onto baking sheet, spacing cookies at least 1 inch apart. Bake in preheated oven 10 to 12 minutes. Cool on baking sheet about 3 minutes; remove to cooling rack.

Standard oven: Preheat to 350°F; bake about 10 minutes.

NUTTY CHOCOLATE CRACKLERS Push a walnut half or whole toasted almond into top of cookie just before baking.

APRICOT KOLACKY

These filled cookies are practically a staple in any Czech household. Use a different flavored filling, if you like.

Makes about 5-1/2 dozen 2-inch pastries
1/2 pound (2 sticks) unsalted butter or margarine, softened
2 packages (3 ounces each) cream cheese, softened
2 cups unbleached all-purpose flour
2 teaspoons baking powder
1 can (12 ounces) apricot pastry filling
Sifted confectioners' sugar

Bakeware: 1 or more aluminum or black steel baking sheets to fit oven

Preheat convection oven to 350°F. Cream together butter and cream cheese. Stir together flour and baking powder. Gradually stir flour mixture into butter to form dough. Work with hands after half the flour mixture has been added. Shape dough into round patty; refrigerate 1/2 to 1 hour or until it becomes firm. Place on lightly floured pastry board and roll out to a generous 1/8-inch thickness. Use 2-inch round cookie cutter or edge of wine glass to cut dough into rounds. Place on ungreased baking sheet, leaving at least 1 inch of space between rounds. Make slight indentation with 3 fingers on each round. Fill each with about 1 teaspoon apricot filling, spreading in circle almost to edge. Bake in preheated oven 10 to 15 minutes or until golden brown. Cool 5 minutes before removing from baking sheet. Gather up dough scraps and repeat filling and baking. Dust with confectioners' sugar before serving.

Standard oven: Preheat to 350°F; bake 10 to 15 minutes.

FROSTED ROHLICKY (Almond Crescents)

A buttery cookie rolled in confectioners' sugar while still warm. Pack these in decorative boxes for yummy holiday gifts.

Makes about 8 dozen
1/2 pound (2 sticks) unsalted butter or margarine, softened
5 tablespoons granulated sugar
2 teaspoons vanilla extract
1 tablespoon water
1/2 teaspoon salt
2 cups unbleached all-purpose flour
2 cups ground almonds
Sifted confectioners' sugar

Bakeware: 1 or more aluminum baking sheets to fit oven

Preheat convection oven to 300°F. Beat together butter and sugar until light and fluffy. Stir in vanilla and water. Stir salt into flour and add to butter gradually, mixing well after each addition. Stir in almonds. Refrigerate dough about 30 minutes (may be kept covered in refrigerator 2 to 3 days). Using 1/2 tablespoon portions, roll into oblong shapes. Place on lightly greased baking sheet 1 inch apart, bending ends to form crescent shape. Bake in center of preheated oven about 15 minutes or until crescents begin to brown lightly. Remove from oven and roll in confectioners' sugar while still warm.

Standard oven: Preheat to 350°F; bake 15 to 20 minutes.

DESSERTS

CRANBERRIED BAKED APPLES

An autumn favorite, baked apples—here with a tart cranberry tang.

Serves 6
1/2 cup sugar
1/4 cup raisins
1/4 cup chopped pecans
3 whole cloves
1/2 cinnamon stick
1/4 teaspoon ground mace
1 cup cranberry liqueur or cranberry juice
6 large baking apples
About 6 tablespoons Crème Fraîche, page 132 (optional)

Bakeware: One 1-1/2-quart shallow metal or glass baking pan

Preheat convection oven to 350°F. Combine sugar, raisins and pecans. Add cloves, cinnamon stick and mace to cranberry liqueur. Core apples and peel 1 inch of skin from top of each apple. Place apples in greased baking pan and fill apples with raisin mixture. Pour cranberry liqueur over apples, coating each one as you pour. Bake in center of preheated oven 30 to 35 minutes or until apples are tender when pierced with a knife. Serve warm topped with dollops of crème fraîche, if you like.

Standard oven: Preheat to 375°F; bake 35 to 40 minutes.

JIMMY'S SUPERSTAR RICE PUDDING ○

Developed for a veteran superstar who's been eating rice pudding since he began traveling baseball's minor league circuit over 30 years ago, this dessert is a particularly healthful version of an American favorite.

Serves 8 to 10
Soft butter or margarine
3 large eggs
3/4 cup honey
3 cups milk
2 teaspoons vanilla extract
Grated rind of 1 orange (orange portion only)
1/4 teaspoon freshly grated nutmeg
1/4 teaspoon ground cinnamon
2 cups cooked rice
1 cup golden raisins, chopped

Bakeware: 1 glass or metal 2-quart shallow baking pan (12 × 7-1/2 × 2 inches)

Preheat convection oven to 325°F. Grease baking pan with soft butter and set aside. Lightly beat eggs in large mixing bowl; stir in honey, milk, vanilla, orange rind, nutmeg, cinnamon, cooked rice and raisins. Pour into greased baking pan and bake in center of preheated oven 40 to 50 minutes or until knife blade inserted in center comes out clean.

Standard oven: Preheat to 350°F; bake about 1 hour.

BRANDIED FRUIT COMPOTE O

A quick and easy dish that can be served for brunch or dessert.

Serves 8 (1/2-cup servings)
One 20-ounce can pineapple chunks in
  unsweetened pineapple juice
One 17-ounce can sliced peaches in light syrup
One 16-ounce can pear halves in light syrup
1/2 cup blackberry brandy
1 cup packed brown sugar
1/2 cup lemon or orange juice
Grated rind of 1 orange (orange portion only)
2 tablespoons butter or margarine, cut into
  small pieces

Bakeware: One 2-quart shallow metal or glass baking pan

Preheat convection oven to 325°F. Drain fruits; reserve 1/2 cup of fruit juices. Arrange fruits in baking pan. Stir together reserved fruit juice; blackberry brandy, brown sugar, lemon juice and orange rind. Pour over fruits. Dot with butter pieces. Bake in preheated oven 20 to 25 minutes. Serve hot as a brunch dish. For dessert, chill and serve over pound cake, topped with whipped cream, or over ice cream.

Standard oven: Preheat to 350°F; bake about 30 minutes.

INDIVIDUAL CRÈME CARAMELS ☆

A light, classic French dessert that may be made a day in advance.

Serves 6
1/4 cup sugar
2 teaspoons vanilla extract
3 cups milk
8 egg yolks
6 tablespoons sugar
6 tablespoons water

Bakeware: Six 1/2-cup ceramic ramekins; 1 or 2 shallow metal baking pans (if ramekins do not fit in 1 baking pan with 1 inch of space all around, place in 2 pans and bake on 2 levels)

Preheat convection oven to 325°F. Stir 1/4 cup sugar and vanilla into milk in medium saucepan. Gently heat to just under the boiling point and remove from heat and cool 10 minutes. In large mixing bowl, whisk egg yolks to blend. Slowly pour hot milk into yolks, whisking constantly to prevent yolks from cooking. Set aside. Stir together 6 tablespoons sugar and water in small saucepan. Bring to a boil over medium heat and allow to boil until syrup turns a golden caramel color, swirling pan occasionally. Place double layer of paper toweling in bottom of shallow baking pan. Place ramekins in pan on paper toweling with 1 inch of space between ramekins. Working quickly, spoon the caramelized sugar into the ramekins and let cool until set, about 5 minutes.

Skim foam from top of reserved milk mixture. Stir gently and ladle into ramekins. Pour hot tap water into baking pan so it comes halfway up sides of ramekins. Place baking pan in center of preheated 325°F oven. Turn temperature down to 300°F and bake 40 minutes or until thin knife blade inserted in center of custard comes out clean. Remove crème caramels from oven and cool to room temperature. Serve as is or refrigerate 2 to 3 hours before serving. To serve unmolded, run thin knife blade around custard, set small dessert plate over ramekin, invert and carefully lift off ramekin. Each crème caramel will have a caramel top and be sitting in a pool of syrup.

Standard oven: Preheat to 350°F; do not reduce temperature, and bake 40 to 45 minutes.

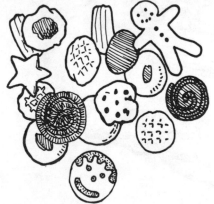

RASPBERRY FLAN

A luscious dessert with a beautiful mauve color and distinctive raspberry fragrance.

Serves 10 to 12

SYRUP
6 tablespoons sugar
6 tablespoons water
3 to 4 drops red food coloring (optional)

CUSTARD
2 packages (10 ounces each) frozen
    raspberries, thawed
6 egg yolks
3 tablespoons cornstarch
1/4 cup sugar
1 cup half-and-half or light cream
1-1/2 teaspoons vanilla extract

Bakeware: One 8-inch round aluminum cake pan; 1 shallow baking pan to accommodate cake pan and fit oven.

To make syrup, combine sugar, water and food coloring in small heavy saucepan. Bring to a boil over medium heat, swirling gently occasionally to mix. Boil about 5 minutes or until syrup begins to turn darker red. Immediately pour into cake pan and tilt to distribute syrup evenly over bottom of pan. Refrigerate to set, about 15 minutes.

Preheat convection oven to 325°F. To make custard, put raspberries through fine blade of food mill or press through sieve to remove seeds. There will be about 2 cups of raspberry purée. In large mixer bowl, beat egg yolks until thick and lemon colored. Stir cornstarch into sugar and beat into egg yolks until mixture is pale and thick. Stir in half-and-half, vanilla and raspberry purée. Pour into prepared pan; place cake pan in shallow baking pan. Pour boiling water into baking pan until it comes halfway up the side of the cake pan. Bake in center of preheated oven 35 to 45 minutes or until knife blade inserted 1 inch from edge comes out clean. Turn off oven and leave flan in oven 10 minutes. Cool at room temperature to lukewarm, then cover and refrigerate until cold, about 2 hours. To unmold slide thin knife blade around edge of flan, invert onto serving platter and lift off cake pan. Flan will be ringed by a pool of pink syrup. Cut in wedges to serve.

Standard oven: Preheat to 350°F; bake about 1 hour.

HOT LEMON SOUFFLE

A soufflé the classic French way with a slightly soft center.

Serves 6
Soft unsalted butter or margarine
Sugar
4 tablespoons (1/2 stick) unsalted butter or margarine
1/2 cup sugar
Grated rind of 2 lemons (yellow portion only)
6 tablespoons lemon juice
4 eggs, separated
1 egg white
1/8 teaspoon cream of tartar
Sifted confectioners' sugar

Bakeware: One 6-cup metal charlotte mold or ceramic soufflé dish

Preheat convection oven to 400°F. Butter the charlotte mold, sprinkle with sugar and tap out excess. Set aside. In a small saucepan, heat 4 tablespoons butter, 1/4 cup of the sugar, lemon rind and lemon juice until butter and sugar melt. Remove from heat and stir in egg yolks 1 at a time. Heat gently, stirring constantly until mixture thickens to the consistency of heavy cream. Remove from heat and cover with a round of waxed paper placed directly on top of mixture until ready to use. (This custard mixture will keep covered at room temperature for 3 to 4 hours.)

Beat 5 room-temperature egg whites until foamy, add cream of tartar and continue beating until soft peaks form. Gradually add remaining 1/4 cup sugar and continue beating until stiff peaks form. Fold warm lemon mixture into stiff egg whites. If necessary, gently heat lemon mixture to warm. Spoon into prepared mold. Place mold in preheated oven, turn temperature down to 375°F and bake 15 to 18 minutes or until soufflé is puffed and brown and pick inserted in center comes out lightly coated (time may have to be increased when using ceramic soufflé dish). For a drier soufflé, bake until pick comes out clean. Sprinkle with confectioners' sugar. Serve immediately.

Standard oven: Preheat to 425°F; turn temperature down to 400°F and bake 15 to 18 minutes.

INDIVIDUAL MOCHA SOUFFLES

Individual soufflés are an impressive dessert for a small special dinner party. Soufflés must be served straight from the oven but they can be assembled and kept at room temperature 30 to 40 minutes before baking.

Serves 4
Soft butter or margarine
2 tablespoons sugar
1/4 cup semisweet chocolate chips
2 tablespoons coffee liqueur
1 tablespoon instant espresso coffee powder
   (available at gourmet shops)
1 teaspoon grated orange rind (orange portion
   only)
5 egg yolks, at room temperature
1/2 cup sugar
6 egg whites, at room temperature
1/8 teaspoon cream of tartar
1/2 cup whipping cream

Bakeware: Four 2-cup individual ceramic soufflé dishes

Preheat convection oven to 400°F. Grease soufflé dishes with soft butter, add 1-1/2 teaspoons sugar to each dish and swirl to coat bottom and sides evenly. Set aside. Stir chocolate chips, coffee liqueur, coffee powder and orange rind in small heavy saucepan over low heat until chocolate melts. Cool to lukewarm. Beat egg yolks and 1/2 cup sugar in medium mixing bowl until very thick and lemon-colored. Pour chocolate mixture slowly into egg yolks, beating all the while. In separate bowl, beat egg whites until foamy, add cream of tartar and continue to beat until stiff peaks form. *Do not* allow whites to become dry. Pour chocolate mixture over egg whites and fold together with rubber spatula. Divide mixture evenly among the prepared soufflé dishes (dishes will be full to within 1/2 inch of top) and smooth the tops. Place soufflés on oven rack with at least 1 inch of space between dishes and slide into preheated oven so soufflés are centered and have "head room" for rising. Bake 12 to 15 minutes or until soufflés are puffed and brown and a cake pick inserted in the center of soufflé comes out clean. While soufflés are baking, whip cream until soft peaks form. To serve, place each soufflé dish on dessert plate and pass whipped cream in sauceboat. Spoon cream over soufflé after breaking soufflé open with dessert spoon.

Standard oven: Preheat to 425°F; bake about 15 minutes.

PIES AND CAKES

FRESH STRAWBERRY PIE

Who can resist fresh strawberries? Orange juice brings out the berry flavor in this easy-to-make version of an American classic. Simple enough for family, fancy enough for company.

Makes one 9-inch pie
1 baked 9-inch pie crust, page 136
1 pint strawberries
3 tablespoons cornstarch
3/4 cup orange juice
1 cup sugar
2 teaspoons lemon juice
1 to 2 drops red food coloring (optional)
1 cup whipping cream, whipped

Cool pie shell. Wash and hull strawberries. Purée half the berries in food processor or blender. In medium saucepan, stir together cornstarch and a few tablespoons orange juice until cornstarch dissolves. Add remaining orange juice, sugar and puréed berries. Stir over medium heat until mixture is clear and thick, about 5 minutes. Stir in lemon juice and food coloring. Cool about 10 minutes, stirring occasionally. Fold in remaining berries. Pour into baked pie shell. Refrigerate at least 4 hours before serving. Serve wedges topped with whipped cream.

STREUSEL PEACH PIE

Streusel-topped pies are the best kind for convection baking.

Makes one 9-inch pie

TOPPING
1/2 cup packed brown sugar
1/2 cup all-purpose flour
1/4 teaspoon ground cinnamon
5 tablespoons unsalted butter or margarine

FILLING
1/2 cup granulated sugar
1 tablespoon cornstarch
Grated rind of 1 lemon (yellow portion only)
4 cups sliced fresh peaches or thawed frozen
   unsweetened sliced peaches

1 unbaked 9-inch pie crust, page 135

Bakeware: One 9-inch metal pie pan

Preheat convection oven to 400°F. To make topping, mix together brown sugar, flour and cinnamon; cut in butter until mixture is crumbly. Set aside. Stir together sugar, cornstarch and lemon rind and toss with sliced peaches. Spoon peaches into unbaked pie shell. Sprinkle topping over peaches, covering completely. Place pie in center of preheated oven, reduce temperature to 375°F and bake 40 to 45 minutes or until crust is brown and topping is crispy.

Standard oven: Preheat to 425°F; bake 40 to 45 minutes.

FRUIT TART WITH PASTRY CREAM

This pastry cream is a particularly light one I learned from master baker John Clancy, one of America's great chefs. The cold whipped cream sets up the custard.

Serves 8
1/2 recipe French Pastry Dough, page 136

PASTRY CREAM
2 tablespoons sugar
4 teaspoons all-purpose flour
Pinch salt
2 teaspoons unflavored gelatin
1 large egg
1/2 cup hot milk
1/2 teaspoon vanilla extract
1/2 cup whipping cream, chilled

About 2 cups whole hulled strawberries or sliced peeled fresh fruit such as peaches, plums, nectarines or grapes

GLAZE
1/2 cup apricot preserves
1 teaspoon Grand Marnier or Cointreau

Bakeware: One 9-inch aluminum tart pan with removable sides

Preheat convection oven to 400°F. Roll out French Pastry Dough on lightly floured surface to 1/8-inch thickness. Roll up on rolling pin, unroll over tart pan and ease into pan. Cut dough to size by rolling pin along top edge of pan. With index finger, push dough up and into each groove along inside edge so dough comes up over pan edge at least 1/8 inch. Then gently bend each "peak" out over pan edge slightly to prevent dough from shrinking below pan edge. Refrigerate dough about 10 minutes to firm. Prick bottom and sides with fork. Press circle of waxed paper against bottom and sides, fill with dried beans or rice and refrigerate another 10 minutes. Bake in center of preheated oven 10 to 12 minutes, remove beans and waxed paper, return to oven and bake another 10 to 15 minutes or until sides and bottom of shell are golden brown and crisp. If bottom of shell bubbles, pierce with fork to deflate. After removing from oven, if bottom of shell is still not brown and crisp, remove from tart pan, place directly on oven rack and bake another 5 minutes. Cool completely.

To make pastry cream, in heavy small saucepan, combine sugar, flour, salt and gelatin. Beat in egg with wooden spoon until smooth. Slowly whisk the hot milk into the egg mixture and heat over medium heat, whisking constantly until mixture comes to boil. Immediately pour through a sieve into a medium mixing bowl, stir in vanilla extract and cool at room temperature to room temperature. *Do not* refrigerate. When custard mixture is cool, whip chilled whipping cream in chilled bowl with chilled beaters until soft peaks form. Fold into custard and immediately pour into baked, cooled tart shell. Top with whole hulled strawberries (hulled ends down) or sliced peeled fruit in attractive pattern.

Let tart set at room temperature while making glaze: Bring apricot preserves to a boil in small saucepan, pour through sieve, working with spoon if necessary, and add Grand Marnier. Cool until syrupy and no longer hot to the touch and brush over fruits. Refrigerate tart until 1/2 hour before serving time.

LATTICE-TOP APPLE PIE

A pre-cooked filling and easy-to-work pie dough make for a picture-perfect pie.

Makes one 9-inch pie

FILLING

3 pounds Granny Smith or Golden Delicious apples, peeled and cored
1/2 cup sugar
1/2 cup water
1 tablespoon grated lemon rind (yellow portion only)
Juice of one lemon
1 teaspoon ground cinnamon
1/4 teaspoon freshly grated nutmeg
1 tablespoon cornstarch

2 recipes Basic Pie Dough, page 135

Bakeware: One 9-inch aluminum pie pan

To make filling, cut apples into chunks and place in 3-quart saucepan. Stir in sugar, water, lemon rind and juice, cinnamon and nutmeg. Bring to a boil, cover and simmer 10 to 15 minutes or until apples are tender but not mushy. Simmer uncovered another 10 minutes or until juices thicken. Remove from heat and cool to room temperature. For fast cooling, spread filling in a large jelly roll pan. When filling is cool to the touch, stir in cornstarch.

To assemble pie, roll out 1 recipe Basic Pie Dough on lightly floured surface to thickness of 1/8 inch. Roll up on rolling pin and unroll over pie pan. Ease into pan and trim dough 1/2 inch larger than pie pan. Pour filling into pie shell and distribute evenly. Roll out remaining pie dough recipe to a thickness less than 1/8 inch. With pastry cutter, cut eight 3/4-inch-wide strips. Lay 4 strips across pie evenly spaced. Wet edge under strip with cold water and gently press strip to edge. Trim away excess strips even with dough edge. Repeat with remaining 4 strips laid diagonally across the first 4 strips. Fold edge in all around and pinch edge with a pastry crimper or press edge with the tines of a fork. If dough softens and becomes difficult to work with at any time, refrigerate 10 to 15 minutes before proceeding. To stabilize edge design, refrigerate 10 minutes before baking. Preheat side-fan convection oven to 400°F and top-fan convection oven to 375°F and bake pie in center of oven 30 to 40 minutes or until crust is brown and crisp. If crust browns too quickly, leaving bottom undercooked, reduce heat by 25 degrees and increase baking time as needed.

Standard oven: Preheat to 425°F; bake 30 to 40 minutes.

APPLE-ORANGE CRISP

An easy dessert that can be made with fresh fruits year round.

Serves 6
2/3 cup packed brown sugar
1/2 cup all-purpose flour
1/2 cup rolled oats
1/3 cup flaked coconut
3/4 teaspoon ground cinnamon
1/2 teaspoon freshly grated nutmeg
Pinch of ground cloves
5 tablespoons soft butter or margarine
3 cups sliced peeled Golden Delicious apples
1 cup orange segments, membrane removed
Soft butter or margarine
Whipping cream or half-and-half (optional)

Bakeware: One 8-inch square metal or glass baking pan

Preheat convection oven to 325°F. Stir together dry ingredients, add butter and mix until crumbly. Toss two thirds of this mixture with apple slices and orange segments. Grease baking pan with soft butter and pour apple mixture into pan. Sprinkle remaining crumbly mixture over the top and bake in center of preheated oven 20 to 30 minutes or until topping is brown and apples are tender when pierced with a fork. Serve warm with cream, if desired.

Standard oven: Preheat to 375°F; bake 30 to 35 minutes.

FREE-FORM APPLE TART ☆

No fancy crust to shape here—just the simplest and most delicious apple tart you'll ever taste. If the all-butter dough becomes difficult to handle at any time, simply refrigerate 10 to 15 minutes to firm before proceeding.

Makes one 9 × 13-inch tart or two 5 × 9-inch tarts

PASTRY DOUGH
2 cups unbleached all-purpose flour
1/4 teaspoon salt
2 teaspoons sugar
6 ounces (1-1/2 sticks) very cold unsalted butter, cut into 1/4-inch dice
1/3 cup ice water

5 to 6 medium Golden Delicious or Rome Beauty apples
6 to 8 tablespoons sugar
1 to 2 tablespoons unsalted butter, cut in small pieces

Crème Chantilly, page 133 (optional)

Bakeware: 1 aluminum or black steel 14 × 17-inch baking sheet, or 2 smaller sheets to fit oven

Preheat convection oven to 375°F. To make dough, pour flour, salt and sugar into bowl, then stir and add butter. Work with fingertips, pastry cutter or fork until butter is about the size of peas. Add ice water a tablespoon at a time and work with fork, then hands, until dough forms a ball. You may have to use more or less water to form a ball. Flatten into rectangular shape, wrap in clear plastic and place in refrigerator to rest 1/2 to 1 hour. (Dough can be frozen at this point and kept in freezer up to 2 months. Remove to refrigerator section 1 day before using.) Remove from refrigerator and leave at room temperature about 5 minutes. On lightly floured pastry board, roll out to 12 × 16-inch rectangle. Transfer dough to baking sheet by rolling onto rolling pin and unrolling over sheet. If making 2 tarts, cut rolled dough in half to make two 8 × 12-inch rectangles and transfer to 2 baking sheets.

To fill and bake, peel, core and cut apples in half vertically. Cut into 1/8-inch-thick lengthwise slices. Arrange overlapping slices on dough in tile-roof pattern, leaving 1-1/2-inch edge of dough empty all around. Fold edge in over apples; seal corners by brushing with cold water and pressing gently. Sprinkle sugar over apples and dot with butter. Bake in preheated oven 40 to 50 minutes or until crust is crisp and golden and apples are tender. Serve warm or at room temperature. If desired, top each serving with a spoonful of Crème Chantilly.

Standard oven: Preheat to 325°F; bake 55 to 60 minutes.

GEORGIA DERBY PIE

A chocolaty kin to the South's more famous pecan pie.

Makes one 9-inch pie
One 9-inch unbaked pie shell, page 135
1/2 teaspoon instant coffee granules
2 tablespoons bourbon whiskey
1/2 cup chopped walnuts or pecans
1/2 cup sugar
2 eggs
1/2 cup white corn syrup
4 tablespoons (1/2 stick) butter or margarine, melted
1 teaspoon vanilla extract
1/2 cup semisweet chocolate chips
Crème Chantilly, page 133 (optional)

Bakeware: One 9-inch aluminum pie pan

Preheat convection oven to 400°F. Prick bottom of pie shell. Bake in preheated oven 3 to 4 minutes or only until crust begins to dry. Remove and cool while making filling. Reduce oven temperature to 325°F. Dissolve instant coffee in bourbon over very low heat. Pour over nuts, stir and set aside. Beat sugar and eggs until well blended. Beat in corn syrup, melted butter and vanilla. Stir in chocolate chips and nuts. Pour filling into pie shell and bake in center of 325°F oven 30 to 40 minutes or until filling is golden and firm and crust is lightly browned. Cool completely before serving. Top each slice with dollop of Crème Chantilly, if desired.

Standard oven: Preheat to 425°F; bake empty pie shell 4 to 5 minutes, reduce oven temperature to 350°F and bake filled pie 40 to 45 minutes.

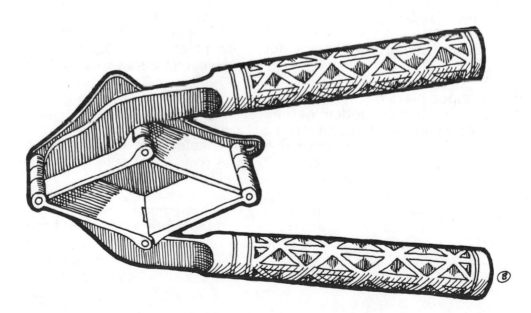

POPPY SEED SOUR CREAM CAKE

May be served as coffeecake or dessert.

Makes one 9-inch tube cake
Soft butter or margarine
1 cup unsalted butter or margarine, softened
1-1/2 cups sugar
1 can (12 ounces) poppy seed pastry filling
5 eggs, separated and at room temperature
1 teaspoon grated lemon rind (yellow portion only)
1 tablespoon lemon juice
1 teaspoon vanilla extract
1 cup sour cream
1/2 cup finely chopped toasted almonds
2 cups sifted unbleached all-purpose flour
1 teaspoon baking soda
1/2 teaspoon salt
1/8 teaspoon cream of tartar
Sifted confectioners' sugar

Bakeware: One 9-inch metal tube pan or bundt pan

Cut doughnut-shaped piece of cooking parchment or waxed paper to fit in bottom of tube pan. Grease tube pan with soft butter and place parchment in bottom of pan. Preheat convection oven to 325°F. In large bowl, cream 1 cup butter and sugar until light and fluffy. Beat in poppy seed filling and then egg yolks 1 at a time, beating well after each addition. Stir in lemon rind, lemon juice, vanilla extract, sour cream and almonds. Sift together flour, baking soda and salt; add to poppy seed mixture one third at a time, beating well after each addition. In separate bowl, beat egg whites until foamy, add cream of tartar and beat until stiff peaks form. Whites should not be dry. Fold egg whites into poppy seed batter, pour into prepared tube pan and smooth top. Bake in center of preheated oven 45 to 50 minutes or until pick inserted in center of batter comes out clean. Cool 5 minutes in cake pan on cooling rack. Unmold cake by running thin spatula around cake edges and inverting onto cooling rack. Just before serving, sprinkle liberally with confectioners' sugar and transfer to serving platter.

Standard oven: Preheat to 350°F; bake about 1 hour.

CREAMY CHEESECAKE ☆

Cheesecake is just about everyone's favorite. This one is quite rich and can be dusted with confectioners' sugar and topped with fresh sweetened fruit when served.

Serves 10 to 12

CRUST
1 tablespoon soft butter or margarine
A scant 1-1/2 cups graham cracker crumbs
1/4 cup sugar
3/4 teaspoon ground cinnamon
1/8 teaspoon freshly grated nutmeg
6 tablespoons unsalted butter or margarine, melted and cooled to room temperature

FILLING

2 packages (8 ounces each) cream cheese, softened
1 cup sugar
3 tablespoons all-purpose flour
4 large eggs, separated and at room temperature
1-1/3 cups sour cream or Crème Fraîche, page 132
1-1/2 teaspoons vanilla extract
1 tablespoon grated lemon rind (yellow portion only)
2 teaspoons lemon juice
1/8 teaspoon cream of tartar

Sifted confectioners' sugar
2 cups sliced strawberries, peaches or nectarines, blueberries or a combination of these, mixed with 2 tablespoons sugar (optional)

Bakeware: One 9-inch aluminum springform pan

To make crust, grease bottom and sides of springform pan with soft butter. Stir together graham cracker crumbs, sugar, cinnamon and nutmeg. Add cooled melted butter and stir with fork to coat all crumbs. Pour crumbs into springform pan and press to bottom and sides of pan so bottom crust is twice as thick as sides. Crumbs should go 2 to 2-1/2 inches up side of pan. Refrigerate while making filling.

Preheat convection oven to 325°F. To make filling, in large bowl, beat cream cheese until fluffy. Stir together sugar and flour, add to cream cheese and beat until blended. Beat in egg yolks 1 at a time; stir in sour cream, vanilla, lemon rind and lemon juice. In a separate bowl, beat egg whites until foamy, add cream of tartar and beat until stiff peaks form. *Do not* overbeat—whites should be stiff and still slightly creamy, not dry. Stir about one third of the whites into cream cheese mixture, then pour cream cheese mixture over remaining whites. With a rubber spatula, fold cream cheese into whites until smooth. Pour into prepared crust and bake in center of prerheated oven 45 to 55 minutes or until top is brown and pick inserted in center comes out slightly gooey. Top of cake may crack; do not be alarmed: This is characteristic of this recipe. Turn off oven and leave cake in oven 30 minutes. Remove to wire rack and let cool to room temperature. Cover and refrigerate at least 2 hours before serving. To serve, sprinkle top of cheesecake with confectioners' sugar and cut into wedges. Top each wedge with a spoonful of fruit, if desired.

Standard oven: Preheat to 350°F; bake about 1 hour or until top is golden and pick inserted in center comes out slightly gooey. Let cheesecake cool in oven 45 minutes, remove and cool to room temperature.

LIME MERINGUE CHEESECAKE ☆

A multi-layered dessert that takes time to prepare, but its blending of tart, sweet and crunchy is worth the effort.

Serves 8 to 10

CRUST
About 1 tablespoon soft butter or margarine
1 cup graham cracker crumbs
3 tablespoons sugar
1/4 teaspoon freshly grated nutmeg
4 tablespoons (1/2 stick) unsalted butter or margarine, melted and cooled to room temperature

CHEESE LAYER
1 package (8 ounces) cream cheese, softened
1/2 cup sugar
2 eggs

LIME LAYER
6 tablespoons unsalted butter or margarine
6 tablespoons sugar
1/2 cup fresh lime juice (juice of about 4 limes)
Grated rind of one lemon (yellow portion only)
3 egg yolks (reserve 2 whites for Meringue Topping)
2 drops each green and yellow food coloring (optional)

MERINGUE TOPPING
2 egg whites, at room temperature
1/4 teaspoon cream of tartar
1/4 cup sugar
1/2 teaspoon vanilla extract

Bakeware: One 8-inch aluminum springform pan

Preheat convection oven to 325°F. To make crust, grease bottom and sides of springform pan with soft butter. Mix together graham cracker crumbs, sugar, nutmeg and melted butter. Pat mixture onto bottom and sides of springform pan. To make cheese layer, beat together cream cheese and 1/2 cup sugar until light and fluffy. Beat in 2 eggs. Pour cream cheese mixture over crust. Bake in center of preheated oven 15 minutes or until knife blade inserted in center comes out clean. Cool.

To make lime layer, in small saucepan over low heat stir together 6 tablespoons unsalted butter, 6 tablespoons sugar, lime juice and lemon rind until butter melts and sugar dissolves. Remove from heat and stir in egg yolks 1 at a time. Add food coloring and stir over low heat until mixture thickens slightly. Pour over cooled cheese layer and let sit at room temperature while the cheesecake sets, about 1 hour. (*Note:* Cake may be prepared to this point 1 day ahead. Cover with plastic wrap and refrigerate. Bring to room temperature before adding meringue topping.)

Preheat convection oven to 325°F. To make meringue, beat egg white until foamy. Add cream of tartar and continue beating, adding sugar gradually until all sugar is incorporated and stiff glossy peaks form. Beat in vanilla. Spread over lime layer, making sure meringue is sealed to crumb-lined edge of pan. Bake in preheated oven about 10 minutes or until meringue is light brown. Cool 2 hours before serving. Remove sides of springform pan. Cut cake into wedges. For easy serving, dip knife in warm water before cutting each slice.

Standard oven: Preheat to 350°F and bake crust and cheese layer 20 minutes; preheat to 350°F and bake meringue about 10 minutes.

THE ULTIMATE CHOCOLATE CAKE ☆

This sinfully delicious single-layer cake is an American version of a French cake taught to me by my wonderful teacher Simone "Simca" Beck. It is a cross between a cake and a mousse and will be the favorite dessert of chocolate fiends everywhere.

Serves 8 to 10
2 tablespoons unsalted butter or margarine, melted and cooled to room temperature
4 eggs, separated
1 package (12 ounces) semisweet chocolate chips*
2 tablespoons instant coffee granules
3 tablespoons water
10 tablespoons (1-1/4 sticks) soft unsalted butter or margarine, at room temperature
2 tablespoons cointreau or orange juice
Pinch of salt
1/2 cup sugar
1/2 cup cornstarch

CHOCOLATE ICING AND GARNISH
18 blanched whole almonds
2/3 cup reserved chocolate chips from cake
1 tablespoon orange juice
1 tablespoon unsalted butter or margarine

Crème Chantilly, page 133 (optional)

Bakeware: One 9-inch springform pan or other high-sided 9-inch cake pan; 1 baking sheet to fit oven

Preheat convection oven to 325°F. Cut a circle of waxed paper to fit bottom of springform pan. Brush bottom of pan with cooled melted butter, place waxed paper circle in pan and brush paper and sides of pan with melted butter. Place egg whites in large bowl and allow to come to room temperature. Reserve 2/3 cup chocolate chips for icing. Melt remaining chocolate with coffee granules and water in heavy-bottomed saucepan over low heat, stirring with wooden spoon until mixture is smooth. Remove from heat and stir in egg yolks 1 at a time. Stir in butter 1 tablespoon at a time. If mixture cools so butter cannot blend in easily, return to very low heat briefly, stirring constantly. Stir in cointreau and set aside.

Beat room-temperature egg whites with pinch of salt until soft peaks form. Gradually add sugar and cornstarch and continue beating until stiff peaks form. Fold warm melted chocolate mixture into whites. Pour batter into prepared springform pan. Bake in preheated oven about 25 minutes or until knife blade inserted in center comes out lightly coated. Center of cake should be soft but not raw. Do not be alarmed if cake cracks slightly. Cake will rise while baking and deflate while cooling. Cool in pan 10 minutes. Run spatula around cake and invert onto serving plate as you would unmold a cake baked in a regular cake pan. Cool completely before icing.

To ice and garnish, preheat convection oven to 325°F. Place almonds on baking sheet with space between nuts and bake in preheated oven 6 to 8 minutes or until golden brown. Cool. To make icing, stir together reserved 2/3 cup chocolate chips, 1 tablespoon orange juice and 1 tablespoon butter over low heat until smooth. Cool 5 minutes. Pour over cooled cake and spread over top with spatula, letting icing flow over edge and down sides of cake in random pattern. Garnish top with toasted almonds. Cut into wedges to serve. If desired, top each wedge with a dollop of Crème Chantilly.

Standard oven: To bake cake, preheat oven to 375°F; bake about 30 minutes. To toast almonds, preheat to 350°F; bake 8 to 10 minutes, watchging carefully for scorching.

*Be sure to use real, not imitation, chocolate.

PERFECTION CARROT CAKE O

A cake so rich and moist that it doesn't need frosting, but it is especially nice with a drizzle of Thin Icing.

Makes one 9-inch square cake
1-1/4 cups unbleached all-purpose flour
1 cup sugar
2 teaspoons baking powder
1 teaspoon salt
2 teaspoons ground cinnamon
1/4 teaspoon freshly grated nutmeg
1 tablespoon grated orange rind (orange portion only)
3/4 cup vegetable oil
2 eggs
2 teaspoons vanilla extract
1 cup grated carrots
1 cup raisins
1 cup chopped walnuts or pecans

THIN ICING
1/2 cup sifted confectioners' sugar
1 tablespoon orange juice

Bakeware: One 9-inch square aluminum cake pan

Preheat convection oven to 325°F. Measure all ingredients except carrots, raisins, nuts and ingredients for icing into large mixer bowl of electric mixer. Blend 1 minute at low speed and scrape down sides of bowl. Beat 2 minutes at medium speed. Stir in carrots, raisins and nuts. Pour into greased cake pan. Bake in preheated oven 30 to 35 minutes or until pick inserted in center comes out clean. Cool 20 minutes. To make Thin Icing, stir together confectioners' sugar and orange juice until smooth. Drizzle over cake. Cut into 9 squares.

Standard oven: Preheat to 325°F; bake 40 to 45 minutes.

CARROT BREAD Divide batter equally among 3 greased 5-1/2 × 3-1/4 × 2-inch aluminum or heavy-duty aluminum foil loaf pans. Bake in preheated 325°F convection oven 40 to 45 minutes or until pick inserted in center comes out clean.

Standard oven: Preheat to 325°F; bake 55 to 60 minutes.

SOUTHLAND BOURBON CAKE ☆

An extraordinary cake that is laced with more than a little of the very American whiskey. Definitely company fare, this cake is best when made a day ahead and left to mellow.

Serves 8 to 12

FILLING
6 egg yolks
3/4 cup sugar
5 tablespoons butter or margarine
1/3 cup bourbon whiskey
1 cup chopped pecans
1 cup chopped golden raisins
1 cup shredded coconut

CAKE
1 tablespoon butter or margarine, melted and cooled to room temperature
2 cups unbleached all-purpose flour
1-1/2 cups sugar
3-1/2 teaspoons baking powder
1 teaspoon salt
1/4 pound (1 stick) butter or margarine, softened
2 teaspoons vanilla extract
1 cup milk
4 egg whites, at room temperature

BOURBON SYRUP
1/2 cup water
1/4 cup sugar
2 tablespoons bourbon whiskey

FROSTING
1/2 cup sugar
1/4 cup light corn syrup
2 tablespoons water
2 egg whites
1/8 teaspoon cream of tartar
2 teaspoons lemon juice
1 teaspoon vanilla extract

Bakeware: Two 8-inch round aluminum cake pans

To make filling, beat egg yolks until light and lemon colored. Gradually add sugar and continue to beat until well blended. Melt butter in saucepan over low heat. Stir in egg mixture and bourbon and continue to stir over low heat until thick. Remove from heat and stir in pecans, raisins and coconut. Refrigerate at least 2 hours.

To make cake, preheat convection oven to 325°F. Cut 2 circles of waxed paper to fit bottoms of cake pans. Brush bottom of each cake pan with cooled melted butter, place 1 waxed paper circle in bottom of each pan and brush waxed paper and sides of pans with melted butter. In large mixer bowl, beat together flour, sugar, baking powder, salt, soft butter, vanilla and 2/3 cup of milk at low speed until blended. Add remaining milk and egg whites. Beat at high speed for 2 minutes. Pour batter into prepared cake pans. Bake in preheated oven 25 to 30 minutes or until pick inserted in center of cake comes out clean. Cool 10 minutes. Slide spatula around edge of cake layers. Invert pans on cooling racks to unmold. Gently remove waxed paper from cake. Cool to room temperature. While cake is cooling, make bourbon syrup.

To make bourbon syrup, stir together water and sugar over low heat until sugar is dissolved. Raise heat, bring to a rolling boil and boil 5 minutes. Remove from heat and stir in bourbon. Let cool to lukewarm. Assemble cake before making frosting: Using a serrated knife, cut each cake layer in half horizontally to make a total of 4 layers. Remove filling from refrigerator and stir to soften. Reserve 1/2 cup filling for top of cake. Place 1 layer on serving plate cut side up and drizzle generously with lukewarm bourbon syrup. Top with one third of remaining filling. Repeat with all layers. Spread reserved 1/2 cup of filling in small circle in center of top layer. Set aside while making frosting.

To make frosting, stir together sugar, corn syrup and water in small saucepan. Cover and bring to a rolling boil over medium heat. Remove cover and boil without stirring until mixture registers 242°F on a candy thermometer. While mixture is boiling, beat egg whites with cream of tartar until soft peaks form. Continue beating at medium speed while pouring hot syrup in a very thin stream into egg whites. Beat at high speed until stiff peaks form. Add lemon juice and vanilla and beat one minute more. Spread frosting over sides and top of cake up to edge of filling circle. Let cake mellow at room temperature overnight before serving.

Standard oven: Preheat oven to 350°F; bake layers 35 to 40 minutes.

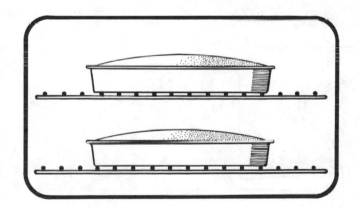

convection
roasting

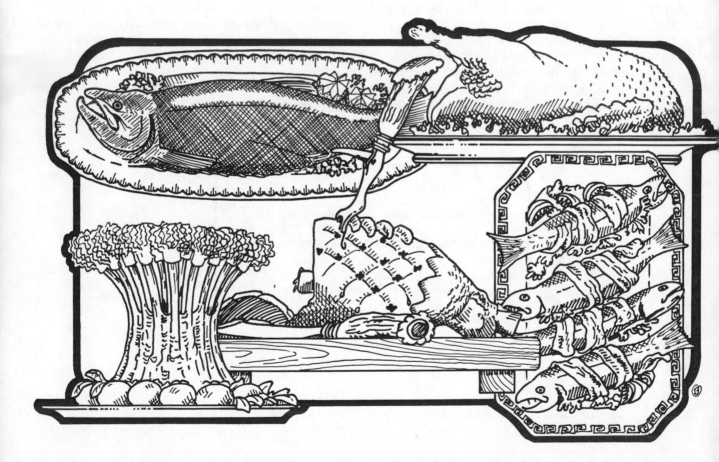

CONVECTION ROASTING VS. STANDARD ROASTING

Not only does the convection oven roast foods in reduced time with reduced energy, but it gives results that are dramatically different from standard roasting. Personally, if a convection oven could do nothing but roast, I would still opt to have one in my kitchen.

To understand convection roasting, it is important to understand roasting in general. Roasting is cooking meat, poultry or other foods by dry heat. To be truly successful, roasting should only be done with tender cuts of meat and tender poultry. The proper conventional method is to place the roast on a rack in a shallow roasting pan and bake it in an oven until the desired internal temperature is reached. Everyone agrees on this basic technique.

But beyond that, there are two schools of thought on roasting. One view holds that meat should be roasted at low temperature (325°F) for maximum juiciness and minimum shrinkage. Another view holds that meat should be seared first in a very hot oven (450°F) for 30 to 60 minutes (depending upon the size of the roast) before reducing the temperature to 325°F for the remainder of the roasting time. The French call this searing action "seizing," which is quite an accurate description. Searing does "seize" the internal juices of the roast, trapping them inside the meat rather than letting them ooze out. Both techniques produce nicely roasted meats, and it is really a matter of preference as to which is best. I would venture to say that people who like rare meat might prefer the searing method.

WHAT MAKES CONVECTION ROASTING DIFFERENT?

With convection roasting, a choice between these two techniques doesn't really have to be made. No matter what temperature a convection oven is set at, the circulating hot air sears the exterior of the roast. This means the initial high-temperature "seizing" step need not be done (except by those who prefer extremely crusty meats and poultry).

In addition to the automatic searing action, convection roasting differs from standard oven roasting in mechanics: In convection roasting, meat, or other food to be roasted, is placed directly on the oven rack and the rack is pushed into the oven so that the food is centered. The drip pan in the bottom of the oven catches the drippings. In other words, the drip pan acts as a roasting pan and the oven rack as a roasting rack.

This is the procedure to follow for basic roasting of any sort, from Standing Rib Roast, page 77, to Oven-roast Potatoes, page 88. There is a time when a standard shallow roasting pan and roasting rack should be used, however—when you wish to make a sauce or gravy directly in the roasting pan, as in, for example, Roast Duckling with Cherry Brandy Sauce, page 85.

DOES WATER HAVE A PLACE IN DRY-HEAT ROASTING?

Most recipes written for roasting will not recommend adding water to the roasting pan. The objection to water is based on the fear that meats will take on a boiled or steamed taste, which could be the case if an excessive amount of water is used.

However, adding a small amount of water to the roasting pan—the drip pan in your convection oven—catches drippings and can make a delicious base for pan juice gravies and sauces.

When using water in roasting, it is important to understand the role of water as a carrier. Water has no flavor of its own; it carries the flavors of whatever goes into it. When used in roasting, water catches the flavorful roast drippings and suspends them so they won't end up as a dried-out blotch on the bottom of the roasting pan.

In convection roasting, it is important to add just enough water to the drip pan to reach a depth of 1/8 to 1/4 inch, and to watch that level during roasting, adding small amounts, if necessary, to maintain at least a film of water and drippings. While the roast is resting, these pan juices should be tasted and seasoned as desired. If you wish to concentrate the flavors, pour juices into a small saucepan and reduce by boiling. If you wish to extend the juices, add the appropriate stock (chicken stock for roast chicken, beef stock for roast beef) and seasonings. The recipes in this chapter give specific directions on when and how to use this delicious by-product of roasting.

SELECTING CUTS FOR ROASTING

All the helpful hints and great cooking techniques won't help one iota if used on the wrong cut of meat. Roasting, more than any other mode of cooking, is abused by cooks who choose the wrong cut of meat, especially beef. Confusion arises because there are many cuts of meat labeled roasts that cannot be roasted successfully.

The best meat for roasting includes only the tenderest (and most expensive) cuts of the animal. Remember that "roast" on a label is a description of the cut, not always the cooking method. Consider the tasty rump roast. It looks lean and meaty and it says "roast"! But don't—roast, that is. Rump roast is actually best when braised (cooked in liquid), which tenderizes it. The only time rump roast should be roasted is when it is a very high quality cut—prime or the best choice—and is cooked to no more than medium rare.

Meat for roasting should be marbled and/or covered with a layer of fat. Meat that is very lean is best when braised (see the "Braising" section). If you wish to roast less tender cuts than those listed below, select top quality meat, cook only to rare or medium rare and cut in thin slices. For best results when roasting, select one of the cuts listed below.

RECOMMENDED CUTS FOR ROASTING

BEEF
Standing rib roast, small and large ends
Rib eye roast, also called Delmonico roast
  (boneless rib eye)
Tenderloin, whole or half,
  also called Chateaubriand roast
Round tip roast ⎰Prime or top quality choice
Top round roast ⎱only; roast only to medium
Rump roast ⎱rare and slice thinly on the
  ⎱diagonal

VEAL
Rib roast
Crown rib roast
Loin roast
Sirloin roast

PORK
Loin end or loin rib roast
Center cut loin roast
Boneless rolled loin roast
Fresh picnic roast, also called picnic shoulder
Shoulder arm roast
Boneless pork shoulder blade
Back ribs
Country-style ribs
Smoked ham, whole, rump half or sirloin half
Smoked pork shoulder, also called smoked
   picnic shoulder

LAMB
Rib roast, also called rack of lamb
Crown roast
Whole shoulder roast
Boneless rolled shoulder roast
Whole leg, shank half of leg or sirloin half of leg
Boneless rolled leg of lamb

POULTRY
Turkey
Chicken
Duck
Cornish hen

MEAT THERMOMETERS

The time recommendations listed in roasting charts are meant as guidelines, never as hard-and-fast rules. By themselves they are not ac-curate enough to give consistently good results. A meat thermometer should always be used. The cost of meat roasts is too high to take chances without one. There are two types you can select: the standard dial-face meat ther-mometer that is inserted in the roast prior to cooking, and the instant-read thermometer that can be inserted in the roast any time during cooking to get a temperature reading in a matter of seconds and then removed.

Either type of thermometer may be used in a convection oven. Be sure the standard ther-mometer dial shows through the oven door while roasting so the door does not have to be opened repeatedly. The instant-read thermom-eter, which may be used for many other foods besides meat, is streamlined and tends to be more accurate than the standard type. How-ever, there is one small drawback to using it to test convection roasts: Each time it punctures the seared, crusty exterior of the roast and is removed, a stream of juices pours from the small hole made by the thermometer. This is not a major problem as long as you control the urge to test the roast every 5 minutes. When using an instant-read thermometer, follow this procedure:

● Determine roasting time by referring to the oven's care-and-use manual, the roasting chart on page 73 and the roasting guidelines, pages 74-75.

● Test the roast when two thirds of the cook-ing time has expired.

● Depending upon the reading, continue to roast or remove the roast to rest before serving.

● If the roast continues to cook, test it at 10- to 15-minute intervals until the desired internal temperature is reached.

INFERNAL INTERNAL TEMPERATURES

In many roasting timetables and on practically all the standard meat thermometers, suggested internal temperatures are given for rare, medium and well done. Unfortunately, many a good roast has been ruined over the years because these figures do not take into consideration the fact that roasted meat continues to cook after leaving the oven. This is why roasts should always be left to "rest" after cooking. Temperatures increase 10 to 15 degrees during resting, which means meat should cook only to within 10 to 15 degrees of the suggested times we always see in print. Turn off the oven when roasts reach the following suggested internal temperatures and then allow the roasts to rest in a warm place (see page 72) for the juiciest, most delicious results you'll ever taste.

TEMPERATURE ON MEAT THERMOMETER BEFORE RESTING

Beef	
Rare	125-130°F
Medium	145-150°F
Well done	155-160°F
Veal	145-150°F
Pork	155-160°F
Smoked Pork	145-150°F
Lamb	
Rare	125-130°F
Medium	145-150°F
Well done	155-160°F
Chicken	165-170°F
Turkey	165-170°F

CONVECTION ROASTING CHART

*In degrees Farenheit, upon leaving oven before roast rests.
**Minutes per pound.

	Weight in Pounds	Temperature Setting	Internal Temperature*			Roasting Time**		
			rare	medium	well done	rare	medium	well done
BEEF								
Standing rib	6-8	350°	125-130°	145-150°	155-160°	16-20	22-25	27-30
Rolled rib	4-6	325°	125-130°	145-150°	155-160°	18-22	23-27	28-32
Rib eye (Delmonico)	4-6	350°	125-130°	145-150°	155-160°	15-18	19-22	23-26
Chuck roast (top quality only)	2-4	350°	130°	140°		17-19	20-22	
Boneless rump or top round or round top roast (top quality only)	3-5	325°	130°	140°		14-17	18-21	
Meatloaf	2-2½	350°		160°			20-30	
PORK (Fresh)								
Bone-in loin	3-7	325°		155-160°			18-22	
Boneless rolled loin	3-5	325°		155-160°			16-20	
Picnic shoulder	4-6	325°		155-160°			24-27	
Crown roast	4-6	325°		155-160°			23-30	
Spareribs	2-4	325°		155-160°			20-30	
SMOKED PORK								
Bone-in ham half, fully cooked	5-7	300° top fan 325° side fan		140°			18-22	
Bone-in ham half, cook-before-eating	5-7	325°		160°			23-27	
Whole ham, fully cooked	10-12	300°		140°			12-15	
Canned ham	5	325°		140°			16-20	
LAMB			rare	medium	well done	rare	medium	well done
Leg, shank or sirloin half, bone-in	3-5	400° (French) 350°	125-130°	140-145° 145-150°	155-160°	15-16	17-18 20-22	23-25
Leg, boneless and rolled	3-6	350°	125-130°	145-150°	155-160°	18-21	22-25	26-30
VEAL				medium	well done		medium	well done
Loin or sirloin	4-6	325°		145-150°	155-160°		20-22	23-25
Shoulder, rolled	4-7	325°		145-150°	155-160°		22-25	26-30
Rib roast	3-5	325°		150-155°			22-27	
POULTRY								
Turkey	10-13	300° top fan 325° side fan		165-170°			12-14	
	14-17			165-170°			15-16	
Turkey breast, boneless	2-4			165-170°			20-25	
Chicken	3-3½	350°		165°			18-24	
Duck	4-5	325°		165°			25-30	
Cornish hen	1-1½ each	350°		165°			45-60	

ON ROASTING PORK

Pork roasts are surely the most misunderstood of all meats. Due to the fear of trichinosis poisoning that still lingers in the hearts and minds of many cooks, pork has been subjected to cruel, unusual and degrading treatment for decades. It all stems from the fear that if not cooked to the proper (safe) degree, pork could make diners seriously ill. The "proper degree" for years was 180° to 185°F, which means cooking pork to the point I call "beyond recognition." At this temperature it is a dried-out tough hunk of grey fiber. Research has disclosed that trichinosis bacteria are killed at 138°F, so it makes much more sense and gives you a better, bigger, juicier product to cook pork to the 155° to 160°F range and then let it rest before carving. Any danger of trichinosis is eliminated, and you will find a whole new appreciation of roasted pork. If you find a trace of pink near the bone, don't be alarmed. As long as your roast was cooked beyond 138°F, it is perfectly safe.

ROASTS CAN BE REGAL

The presentation of a convection-roasted meat or poultry dish to your guests can be a dramatic event. Convection cooking will guarantee a beautiful roast with a minimum of work. Use an interesting, colorful garnish and it will be a platter fit for a king. Here are some garnish suggestions for regal roasts:
● sprigs of parsley with spiced crabapples for beef or pork
● a ring of curly endive with cherry tomatoes around beef or poultry

● orange slices or wedges with ham or any roast that is served with a fruit sauce
● bunches of glazed green grapes around turkey or chicken (see page 138 for recipe)
● Broiled Apricots, page 109, and watercress or sprigs of mint with pork or poultry
● Oven-roast Potatoes, page 88, or other accompanying foods that are part of the menu.

If you wish to impress guests even more, brush up on your carving skills and carve right at the table. There are several good books on carving and it certainly is a skill worth learning not only for presentation purposes but because carving portions properly and efficiently can help stretch your meat dollar.

CONVECTION ROASTING GUIDELINES

● **Reduce Conventional Roasting Time by One Fourth to One Third.** Determine the approximate cooking time by consulting the roasting chart found on page 73 or the roasting recipes in this chapter. To convert a standard roasting time to convection roasting time, reduce the standard time by one third to begin and add time to that if necessary to reach desired doneness.
● **Always Use a Meat Thermometer.** Insert a standard meat thermometer in the roast so the tip does not rest in fat or next to bone. Bones conduct heat and may give an inaccurate reading. Insert an instant-read thermometer in the same way but only after two thirds of the convection cooking time has elapsed to avoid needless loss of natural juices. Follow the recommended internal temperature readings on page 72.

● **Roast Foods Directly on the Oven Rack.** Place the roast directly on the oven rack so that it is centered in the oven leaving at least one inch of air space all around. A roast that touches the walls of the oven is too big for best results.

● **Do Not Use Aluminum Foil to Cover Roasts or Drip Pan.** This may take some getting used to for some of us. For years we have been told to cover roasts with aluminum foil for faster roasting. This should not be done in a convection oven, as aluminum foil placed around a roast will hamper the natural searing action. Aluminum foil that has been placed in the drip pan may get blown around the oven cavity, hampering the air flow.

● **Pan Juices Can Be Made in the Drip Pan.** With some roasts, pan juices can be made in the drip pan. Pour one-half to one cup water in the drip pan during roasting. The water will collect flavorful drippings and may act as a base for a gravy or sauce.

● **Brush Roasts with Glaze or Barbecue Sauce Only During the Last 10 to 20 Minutes of Cooking.** Earlier brushing may cause scorching.

● **Frozen Meats May Be Roasted in a Convection Oven.** Fresh or partially thawed meats will produce a better product than frozen meats, which are difficult to season properly and tricky to time accurately. To roast frozen meats, increase the convection cooking time for un-frozen meat by one third to one half; season the meat and insert a thermometer halfway through cooking time.

● **Always Allow Roasted Meats and Poultry to Rest in a Warm Place After the Desired Internal Temperature Is Reached.** Resting time varies with the size of the roast and the internal temperature—the larger the roast and the higher the temperature, the longer the resting time—but it is usually between 10 and 20 minutes. Resting allows juices to settle evenly and facilitates easy carving. Rest roasts in the turned-off oven with the door slightly ajar, or transfer to a heated platter and cover with aluminum foil.

● **Other Foods May Be Cooked While Roasting.** Any convection oven with two racks can cook other foods while roasting, giving the oven a complete meal capability. Place the roast on the bottom rack over the drip pan; slide shallow casserole pans or whole potatoes for baking on the rack above the roast, leaving at least one inch of air space between roast and top rack. For best results, cook only foods that cook at the same temperature as the roast. Some recommended recipes for cooking on top rack while roasting include Creamy Carrot Casserole, Cheesy Scalloped Potatoes, Oven-roast Potatoes and Baked Potatoes.

MEAT, FOWL AND FISH

GERMAN-STYLE ROASTED RIBS O

This simple dish is especially good served with warm applesauce.

Serves 4
2 to 2-1/2 pounds pork spareribs
1 teaspoon salt
1/2 teaspoon onion powder
1/2 teaspoon lemon pepper
1 tablespoon caraway seeds

Bakeware: 1 or 2 oven racks or 2 jelly roll pans to fit oven

Preheat convection oven to 325°F. To remove membrane from back of rib slab, slide a fork tine under membrane 1 rib away from small end of slab, pull up to loosen membrane, grasp with hand and pull off full length of slab. Mix together salt, onion powder and lemon pepper; rub this mixture on both sides of ribs. Place ribs directly on oven rack, fat side up. If ribs must be roasted in 2 layers, place ribs in jelly roll pans. Sprinkle with caraway seeds. Roast in preheated oven 1 to 1-1/4 hours or until tender.

Standard oven: Preheat to 350°F; roast 1-1/2 hours.

BARBECUED SPARERIBS O

The juiciest ribs you'll ever eat with a minimum of work!

1 or more 1-1/2-pound slabs of pork spareribs (depending on size of oven rack)
Kosher salt
Freshly ground black pepper
1/2 to 1 cup bottled or homemade barbecue sauce
1/2 to 1 tablespoon Dijon-style mustard

Bakeware: 1 oven rack with drip pan in place

Preheat convection oven to 325°F. To remove membrane from back of rib slab, slide a fork tine under membrane one rib away from small end of slab, pull up to loosen membrane, grasp with hand and pull off full length of slab. Rub slab on both sides with salt and pepper. Stir together barbecue sauce and mustard and set aside. Place rib slab(s) on oven rack meaty side up. If cooking more than 1 slab, allow at least 1 inch of space between slabs. Cook slabs only on 1 rack to keep fat from top slab from dripping onto bottom slab. Slide rack into center of preheated oven and roast 45 to 50 minutes. Remove from oven and brush on both sides with barbecue sauce; return to oven and roast 5 to 10 minutes more.

Standard oven: Preheat to 350°F; roast ribs in shallow roasting pan about 60 minutes, brush with barbecue sauce and return to oven for 15 to 20 minutes.

STANDING RIB ROAST WITH YORKSHIRE PUDDING ☆

The ultimate treat for a beef-lover's birthday celebration.

Serves 6 to 8
One 6- to 8-pound standing rib roast, prefer-
  ably from the small end
About 1 tablespoon kosher salt
Freshly ground black pepper

YORKSHIRE PUDDING
1 cup sifted unbleached all-purpose flour
1/2 teaspoon salt
1/4 teaspoon freshly ground black pepper
1 cup milk
2 large eggs
About 4 tablespoons beef drippings

Bakeware: 1 oven rack with drip pan in place;
two 6-cup muffin tins

Preheat convection oven to 350°F. Pat rib roast dry with paper toweling. Rub salt and pepper all over roast and place on oven rack. If using meat thermometer, insert so point rests in center of meat. Slide rack into preheated oven so roast is centered. For rare, roast 16 to 20 minutes per pound or until a meat or instant-read ther-mometer registers 130°F; for medium, roast 22 to 25 minutes per pound or until thermometer registers 150°F; for well done, roast 27 to 30 minutes per pound or until thermometer regis-ters 160°F.

While meat is roasting, make Yorkshire Pud-ding batter: In mixing bowl, stir together flour, salt and pepper. Stir together milk and eggs until well blended. Gradually beat into flour and continue to beat until bubbly. Allow to stand loosely covered at room temperature 20 to 30 minutes. When roast reaches desired degree of doneness, remove to a warm platter, cover and let rest in a warm place about 20 minutes. While roast is resting, bake Yorkshire Pudding: Remove drip pan from oven and raise oven temperature to 425°F. Slide 1 or 2 oven racks into oven (to accommodate two 6-cup muffin tins) and heat muffin tins in oven about 2 minutes. Remove from oven and immediately spoon 1 teaspoon beef drippings into each muffin cup and divide pudding batter equally among the 12 cups, filling each about two thirds full. Bake muffin tins in oven 8 to 10 minutes, reduce oven temperature to 350°F and bake another 8 to 10 minutes or until puddings are puffed, golden and a pick inserted in the center comes out clean. Remove from oven and serve immediately with rib roast. To carve rib roast, cut horizontally along bone, then slice down toward bone.

Standard oven: Preheat to 325°F; roast 23 to 25 minutes per pound for rare (130°F), 27 to 30 minutes for medium (150°F) or 32 to 35 minutes for well done (160°F). Bake Yorkshire Pudding at 450°F for 10 minutes, reduce temperature to 375°F and bake another 10 to 15 minutes.

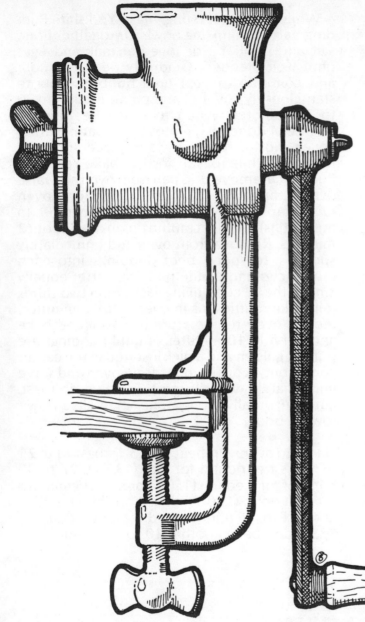

DOWN-HOME GOOD MEATLOAF

This meatloaf can be cooked directly on the oven rack to take full advantage of convection roasting. The outside of the loaf is brown and crusty while the interior stays juicy and tender. As a leftover, this loaf makes wonderful sandwiches.

Serves 6
2 pounds ground beef
1/4 pound salt pork, ground or chopped fine
1 large egg
1 cup dry bread crumbs
1 cup milk
1/2 cup chopped onion
2 teaspoons salt
1/2 teaspoon freshly ground pepper
Flour

Bakeware: 1 oven rack with drip pan in place, or 1 baking sheet

Preheat convection oven to 350°F. Mix all ingredients except flour. Shape into oblong loaf. Dredge lightly with flour and insert meat thermometer so point rests in center of meatloaf. Place on oven rack and slide into preheated oven so meatloaf is centered. If mixture is too soft to hold its shape on rack, refrigerate loaf 30 minutes before placing on rack, or roast on baking sheet. Bake 50 to 60 minutes or until meat thermometer registers 160°F. Remove from oven and let rest 5 to 10 minutes before slicing.

Standard oven: Preheat to 350°F; place meatloaf on roasting rack in shallow roasting pan and bake about 1-1/4 to 1-1/2 hours or until meat thermometer registers 160°F.

ROAST PORK WITH PAN JUICE GRAVY

A simple yet elegant roast. The technique in this recipe can be used with many roasting cuts.

Serves 6 to 8
4 to 5-pound pork loin roast, bone in
About 1 tablespoon kosher salt
1/2 teaspoon freshly ground pepper
1/2 teaspoon dried thyme, crushed
1 cup water

GRAVY
2 to 3 tablespoons dry white vermouth
About 1/2 cup water or chicken or beef stock
Salt and freshly ground pepper
Beef or chicken seasoning base (optional)

Bakeware: Oven rack with drip pan in place

Preheat convection oven to 325°F. Rub pork roast with salt, pepper and thyme. Place on oven rack; insert meat thermometer if desired. Slide rack into center of preheated oven. Roast 18 to 22 minutes per pound or until instant-read or meat thermometer registers 155° to 160°F. After roast has been in oven about 30 minutes, add enough water to drip pan to film bottom and collect pork drippings. Add more water during roasting to keep drippings from scorching. When roast is done, remove to warm platter, cover with aluminum foil and let rest in a warm place while making gravy.

To make gravy, pour contents of drip pan into small saucepan, scraping up any brown bits with wooden spatula. Skim off grease, leaving only brown pork juices in pan. Add dry vermouth and stock, bring to a boil and boil vigorously 5 minutes to reduce and mellow vermouth flavor. Taste and correct seasoning with salt and pepper. If flavor is weak, add small amount of beef or chicken base; if gravy tastes too strong, add small amount of water. To serve, slice the roast and spoon gravy over slices.

Standard oven: Preheat to 350°F; roast 24 to 28 minutes per pound or until a meat or instant-read thermometer registers 155° to 160°F.

HERB-ROASTED CHUCK ROAST ○

A delicious and economical entrée that is juicy and tender when cooked to rare or medium rare.

Serves 6 to 8

3/4 teaspoon each dried thyme leaves,
   rosemary leaves and summer savory
1-1/2 teaspoons salt
1/2 teaspoon freshly ground pepper
1/2 teaspoon paprika
One 3- to 4-pound prime or choice blade chuck
   roast, 1-1/2 to 2 inches thick

Bakeware: 1 oven rack with drip pan in place

Preheat convection oven to 350°F. In mortar with pestle, crush together thyme leaves, rosemary leaves and summer savory. Mix with salt, pepper and paprika. Rub mixture over both sides and edges of chuck roast. If using meat thermometer, insert so tip does not rest in fat or against bone. Place roast on oven rack and slide into center of preheated oven. Roast 18 to 22 minutes per pound or until a meat or instant-read thermometer registers 130°F for rare or 140°F for medium rare. Turn off oven, leave door ajar and let roast rest 5 to 10 minutes before carving. Remove bones and slice meat thin, on the diagonal.

Standard oven: Preheat to 375°F; roast 20 to 24 minutes per pound or until a meat or instant-read thermometer registers 130°F for rare or 140°F for medium rare.

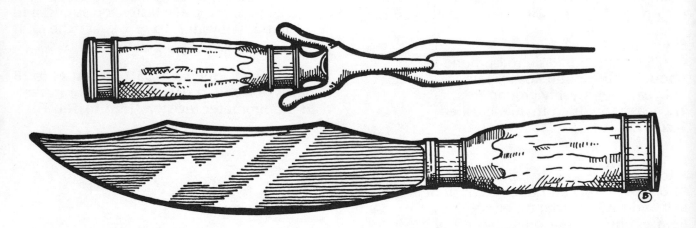

ROAST LEG OF LAMB
WITH BREAD CRUMB DRESSING ○

This is lamb the French way—simple to prepare yet elegant.

Serves 6 to 8
One 3- to 4-pound leg of lamb (shank or sirloin)
2 to 3 garlic cloves, peeled and cut in half
   lengthwise
Olive oil
Kosher salt
Freshly ground black pepper
1/2 to 1 cup water

DRESSING
3 tablespoons unsalted butter or margarine
3 shallots, minced, or 3 tablespoons
   minced onion
2 garlic cloves, crushed
1 cup French bread crumbs, dry or day-old
1/4 teaspoon dried sage

Bakeware: 1 oven rack with drip pan in place

Preheat convection oven to 400°F. Trim away excess fat on lamb. Cut slits in leg and insert a garlic sliver in each slit. Brush lamb with olive oil and rub with salt and pepper. Place lamb on oven rack; insert meat thermometer in thickest part of leg so point does not rest on bone or fat. Slide rack into preheated oven so lamb is centered. Pour about 1/2 to 1 cup water into drip pan in bottom of oven, so that pan is completely coated. As lamb roasts, make sure there is always enough water in drip pan to catch lamb juices. Roast to desired degree of doneness: 15 minutes per pound for rare (130°F internal temperature), 18 minutes per pound for medium (150°F internal temperature), 20 minutes per pound for well-done (170°F internal temperature).

Turn oven off and let lamb rest in oven with door ajar for 15 minutes before carving. While meat is resting, make dressing: Melt butter in frypan. Add shallots and garlic and cook and stir until shallots are tender, 3 to 4 minutes. Add bread crumbs and sage and toss to coat crumbs with butter. If dry crumbs remain, add more butter. Cook over low heat, stirring constantly, about 5 minutes or until crumbs have browned lightly. Pour pan juices from drip pan into small serving bowl and skim off fat. To serve, thinly slice lamb parallel to bone, place on warm serving plate and top with 1 spoon of pan juices and 1 spoon of seasoned bread crumbs.

Standard oven: Preheat to 425°F; follow times listed above.

ROAST CHICKEN WITH TARRAGON CREAM SAUCE ☆

Instead of carving a roast chicken, why not cut it into quarters so that all the succulent meat, even that right next to the bone, can be enjoyed?

Serves 4
About 1/2 cup water
One 3- to 3-1/2-pound roasting chicken or
    broiler-fryer
1 teaspoon fresh minced tarragon, or
    1/2 teaspoon crushed dried tarragon
1 shallot, peeled and quartered, or 1 piece onion
Kosher salt
Freshly ground white pepper
4 tablespoons (1/2 stick) soft unsalted butter or
    margarine
1/4 cup chicken stock
1/4 cup dry white vermouth
1 cup Crème Fraîche, page 132, or whipping
    cream
1 teaspoon lemon juice
Salt
Freshly ground white pepper
1 teaspoon fresh minced garragon, or
    1/2 teaspoon crushed dried tarragon

Bakeware: 1 oven rack with drip pan in place

Pour water into drip pan in oven. Preheat convection oven to 350°F. Pat chicken dry inside and out with paper toweling. Sprinkle tarragon and shallot into chicken cavity. Truss bird with trussing needle and string. Sprinkle with salt and pepper and rub all over with soft butter. Place on oven rack breast side up. Slide rack into preheated oven and roast 45 minutes to 1 hour or until drumstick is loose and instant-read thermometer inserted in meaty portion of drumstick registers 165°F. Remove chicken to a warm platter and keep warm while making the sauce: Pour off drippings from drip pan except for the last 2 to 3 tablespoons and any brown bits that have accumulated. With rubber spatula, scrape these last drippings into 9-inch skillet. Add chicken stock to drip pan to loosen last bits and pour into skillet. Add vermouth, bring to a boil and boil until syrupy, about 5 minutes. Add Crème Fraîche and simmer about 5 minutes or until slightly reduced. Stir in lemon juice, salt and pepper to taste and the tarragon. To serve, cut chicken into quarters with poultry shears and pass sauce in gravyboat.

Standard oven: Preheat to 350°F; roast chicken on rack in shallow roasting pan 1-1/4 to 1-1/2 hours.

CORNBREAD-STUFFED ROAST TURKEY

Add fresh ingredients to cornbread stuffing mix for a delicious dressing that goes together in minutes and makes this turkey a special treat.

CORNBREAD SAUSAGE STUFFING
1 tablespoon butter or margarine
1/2 cup sliced celery
1/4 pound bulk pork sausage
1 package (6 ounces) cornbread stuffing mix
1/2 cup chopped pecans

One 10- to 10-1/2-pound turkey
4 tablespoons (1/2 stick) butter or margarine
1 tablespoon kosher salt
Freshly ground white pepper

GRAVY
4 tablespoons turkey drippings
4 tablespoons all-purpose flour
2 cups turkey or chicken stock
1/2 to 1 teaspoon turkey or chicken seasoning base (optional)

Bakeware: 1 oven rack with drip pan in place

To make stuffing, melt 1 tablespoon butter in medium skillet, add celery and cook over medium heat 2 to 3 minutes. Remove celery with slotted spoon, add sausage to skillet and cook and stir until sausage loses its pink color. Drain off any excess fat. Set aside. Prepare stuffing mix according to package directions. Stir in celery, sausage and pecans.

Preheat convection oven to 300°F for top-fan ovens and 325°F for side-fan ovens. Pat inside and outside of turkey dry with paper towels. Fill turkey cavity loosely with stuffing, truss cavity closed and tie drumsticks together. Tuck wing tips under turkey body and truss neck cavity, filling with any stuffing that may be remaining. Rub turkey on all sides with salt and pepper; brush with melted butter and place on oven rack. If using meat thermometer, insert so that point rests in the part of the thigh next to the body without touching bone. Slide rack into preheated oven so turkey is centered. Roast 2 to 2-1/4 hours or until a meat or instant-read thermometer registers 165° to 170°F, basting with butter 2 or 3 times. Watch drip pan during roasting and add water if drippings begin to dry up. Let turkey rest in turned-off oven 10 minutes. Remove to carving board or platter. Let rest 10 minutes more while making gravy.

To make gravy, pour 4 tablespoons turkey drippings from drip pan into medium saucepan, scraping up any brown bits from bottom of drip pan. Heat and add 4 tablespoons flour and cook and stir over medium heat until mixture bubbles 2 minutes. Remove from heat and whisk in turkey stock. Return to heat and bring to a boil, stirring constantly. Simmer 2 minutes and taste and correct seasonings. If turkey flavor is weak, add 1/2 to 1 teaspoon turkey base. Pour into gravyboat and serve with carved turkey. For a creamy gravy, use 1-1/2 cups stock and 1/2 cup milk or half-and-half in place of 2 cups stock.

Standard oven: Preheat to 325°F; roast 3-1/2 to 4 hours.

GLAZED ROASTED TURKEY BREAST

Boneless turkey breast, which is available fresh and frozen, is an economical cut since it contains no waste and is usually available at a reasonable price. This recipe would also work well on a rotisserie.

Serves 6 to 8
One 2- to 2-1/2-pound boneless turkey breast
Salt
Freshly ground pepper
2 teaspoons Herbes de Provence, page 137
Water (optional)

GLAZE
1/3 cup apricot preserves
1 tablespoon sherry vinegar or red wine vinegar
2 tablespoons water
4 whole cloves
1/2 cinnamon stick
1 tablespoon olive oil
1/2 chicken bouillon cube

Bakeware: 1 oven rack with drip pan in place

Preheat side-fan convection ovens to 325°F, top-fan ovens to 300°F. Pat turkey breast dry with paper toweling. Rub all over with salt and pepper to taste and the Herbes de Provence. Place turkey breast on oven rack, insert meat thermometer so point rests at center of breast and slide rack into center of the preheated oven. Roast 45 to 50 minutes or until a meat or instant-read thermometer registers 165°F to 170°F. If turkey drippings begin to brown during roasting, add water to drip pan to coat lightly. While turkey is roasting, make glaze: Combine all glaze ingredients in small saucepan over medium heat and bring to a boil. Simmer about 5 minutes and remove from heat. After turkey breast has cooked about 30 minutes, baste with glaze. Repeat basting 2 or 3 times during remaining roasting time.

Standard oven: Preheat to 325°F; roast 1 to 1-1/4 hours, basting with glaze during the last 20 minutes of roasting.

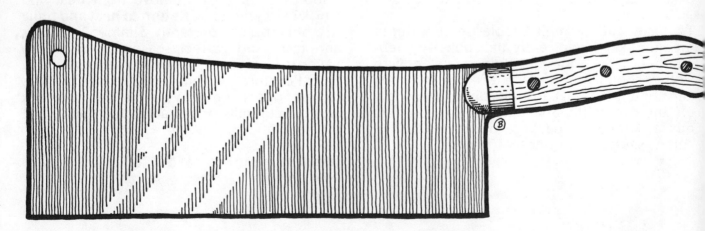

ROAST DUCKLING WITH CHERRY BRANDY SAUCE ☆

This cherry sauce, made with duck stock and laced with brandy, is not sweet but piquant—an ideal complement to the slightly gamey flavor of duck.

Serves 4
One 5-pound fresh or thawed duckling
2 to 3 teaspoons kosher salt
Freshly ground pepper to taste
1 teaspoon dried rosemary leaves
1 cup water
1 can (1 pound) dark pitted cherries
1/2 cup cherry brandy
1-1/2 cups Duck Stock, page 132, or chicken
   stock or a combination of the two
2 teaspoons lemon juice
Salt and pepper to taste
2 tablespoons cornstarch
1/4 cup cold water or stock
2 to 3 tablespoons cherry brandy (optional)

Bakeware: 1 shallow flameproof roasting pan to fit oven; 1 roasting rack

Preheat convection oven to 325°F. Remove giblets from duck and use to make stock, if desired (see page 132). Rub 2 to 3 teaspoons salt and pepper over duck and inside cavity. Sprinkle rosemary inside cavity. Fasten cavity closed with skewers; tie drumsticks together and skewer neck skin in place. Place on roasting rack in flameproof roasting pan, breast side up. Prick skin in several places, making sure to go through skin just into fat, not into meat. Pour 1 cup water into pan. Roast in center of preheated oven 1-1/2 hours, pricking skin occasionally to release excess fat. If level of drippings goes down and exposes pan surface, add more water. Remove duck and rack from pan and pour off drippings, leaving just a film in pan. Return duck and rack to pan. Drain cherries, reserving liquid. Add cherry liquid and cherry brandy to roasting pan. Baste duck with this mixture and continue to roast 20 to 30 minutes or until meat is tender and drumstick moves easily when wiggled.

To make the sauce, remove duck to platter; keep warm in 150°F oven while making sauce. Transfer roasting pan to burner on range, add stock and heat to boiling, scraping up bits from the bottom of the pan. Boil 5 minutes and pour through strainer into saucepan. Add lemon juice and salt and pepper to taste; boil 5 minutes to concentrate flavors. Mix cornstarch with cold water and whisk into sauce gradually until desired consistency is obtained. Add drained cherries and 2 to 3 tablespoons cherry brandy. Simmer 2 minutes. Spoon small amount of sauce over duck; pour remaining sauce into gravyboat. Cut duck in fourths to serve. Nice with wild rice.

Standard oven: Preheat to 350°F; roast 1-1/2 hours, then baste and roast 30 minutes more.

ROAST DUCK WITH GRAVY

There is nothing like the aroma of roast duck to whet the appetite! If your oven will accommodate two ducks, double this recipe to serve eight. Sauerkraut Casserole, page 128, makes a nice accompaniment.

Serves 4
One 4- to 5-pound duck
About 1 tablespoon kosher salt
Freshly ground black pepper
3 or 4 juniper berries
1/2 teaspoon dried rosemary leaves
1/2 bay leaf

GRAVY
2 tablespoons duck drippings
2 tablespoons all-purpose flour
About 1 cup hot Duck Stock, page 132
About 1/2 teaspoon chicken seasoning base
  (optional)

Bakeware: 1 oven rack with drip pan in place

Preheat convection oven to 325°F. Reserve giblets for making stock. Remove excess fat from duck cavity. With paper toweling, pat duck dry inside and out. Sprinkle salt and pepper lightly into cavity, add juniper berries, rosemary leaves and bay leaf. To truss duck, fasten neck and tail openings closed with trussing needle and string or with long wooden picks; tuck wing tips under body. Rub remaining salt and pepper all over duck and place on oven rack. With sharp fork, prick duck all over so fork penetrates skin and fat but not meat. This will help render fat. Slide duck into center of preheated oven and roast 1-1/2 to 2 hours, pricking occasionally to render fat, or until drumstick is loose when wiggled. Remove duck to warm platter and keep warm while making gravy.

To make gravy, pour duck drippings from drip pan, reserving the last 2 tablespoons for the gravy. Pour these 2 tablespoons into a small saucepan, scraping up any brown bits that cling to the drip pan. Rinse drip pan with a small amount of hot stock and reserve. Add 2 tablespoons flour to drippings in saucepan, stir to make a paste and heat to boiling. Boil 2 minutes, remove from heat and add duck stock all at once, including stock in drip pan. Whisk to blend well, bring to a boil and simmer 2 minutes. Taste and correct seasonings. If duck flavor is weak, add chicken base. To serve, cut duck into quarters with poultry shears and pass gravy in gravyboat.

Standard oven: Preheat to 350°F; roast duck on rack in shallow pan 1-1/2 to 2 hours.

BAKED STUFFED FISH

A simple dish that is also colorful and elegant.

Serves 4

STUFFING
4 tablespoons (1/2 stick) butter or margarine
1/2 cup chopped shallots or onion
1/2 cup chopped celery
1/2 cup chopped carrots
1 cup soft bread crumbs (about 2 slices white
    bread torn into pieces)
2 tablespoons milk
2 tablespoons snipped parsley
1/2 teaspoon Herbes de Provence, page 137
1/4 teaspoon salt

2 whole red snappers, about 1 to 1-1/2 pounds
    each, or 1 whole whitefish or lake trout,
    about 3 to 3-1/2 pounds, cleaned and dressed
1/2 teaspoon salt
1/4 teaspoon freshly ground pepper

BASTING SAUCE
2 tablespoons butter or margarine
1 tablespoon lemon juice
1 teaspoon Worcestershire sauce

Bakeware: One 9 × 13 × 2-inch metal or glass baking pan

Preheat convection oven to 325°F. To make stuffing, melt 4 tablespoons butter in medium frypan. Add shallots, celery and carrots. Cook and stir over medium heat until celery is tender, about 5 minutes. Stir in remaining stuffing ingredients; cook and stir 1 to 2 minutes. Sprinkle fish cavity with 1/2 teaspoon salt and pepper. Lightly fill fish cavities with stuffing. Place fish in greased baking pan. Stir together basting sauce ingredients and brush generously over fish. Bake in center of preheated oven 20 to 25 minutes, basting 2 to 3 times. Fish is done when flesh is opaque and flakes easily with a fork.

Standard oven: Preheat to 350°F; bake 25 to 30 minutes.

SIDE DISHES

BAKED POTATOES

This traditional favorite can be baked by itself or at the same time as a roast, braised dish or casserole.

Idaho baking potatoes, about 8 ounces each
Vegetable oil (optional)

Bakeware: 1 oven rack

Preheat convection oven to 375°F (preheating is not necessary but shortens cooking time). Scrub potatoes, pat dry and puncture skin with tines of a fork. For crispy skins, bake potatoes as is; for soft skins, rub potatoes with vegetable oil. Place on oven rack, allowing at least 1 inch of space around each potato. Slide rack into preheated oven and bake 45 to 60 minutes or until until tender. If desired, start potatoes in cold oven and increase baking time by 15 minutes.

To bake potatoes while roasting, place potatoes on same rack with roast or separate rack *above* roast, making sure potatoes have 1 inch of air space all around.

Standard oven: Preheat to 375°F; roast 1 to 1-1/2 hours.

OVEN-ROAST POTATOES

An ideal accompaniment for roasted and grilled meats.

Serves 4 to 6
4 large unpeeled Idaho potatoes
2 tablespoons butter or margarine
1/2 teaspoon Seasoned Salt, page 138
Freshly ground pepper

Bakeware: 1 oven rack or aluminum baking sheet

Preheat convection oven to 400°F. Scrub potatoes well. Cut each potato in half lengthwise, then cut each half lengthwise into 3 or 4 wedges. Melt butter with seasonings. Brush each wedge on all sides with the butter mixture. Arrange wedges on oven racks or cookie sheets leaving 1 inch of space between wedges. Roast in preheated oven 15 to 20 minutes for tender golden-brown wedges, 25 to 30 minutes for crusty brown wedges. If cooking in oven with a roast, use roasting temperature recommended for roast and increase cooking time for potatoes to 30 to 45 minutes.

Standard oven: Preheat to 425°F; follow times listed above.

ROASTED PEPPER SALAD

From the sunny shores of Provence comes a salad that can also be used as a first course. The brilliant combination of green and red makes it a natural for the buffet table when doubled or tripled.

Serves 4
2 large sweet green peppers
2 large sweet red peppers
1/4 cup olive oil
1 tablespoon lemon juice
1-1/2 teaspoons sherry wine vinegar
1/8 teaspoon salt
Freshly ground pepper
2 teaspoons snipped parsley
1 teaspoon fresh minced basil (optional)
4 lettuce leaves

Bakeware: 1 oven rack with drip pan in place

Place peppers on oven rack, leaving at least 1 inch of space between peppers, and slide rack into cold oven. Set temperature control at 375°F and turn on oven. Roast peppers 30 to 40 minutes or until skins look dry and shriveled. Cool peppers on cooling rack 15 minutes, peel, remove seeds and veins, and cut into strips. Flesh should be soft but not mushy. Whisk together olive oil, lemon juice, vinegar, salt and pepper. Add pepper strips, toss and cover. Marinate at room temperature about 1 hour or in refrigerator 2 to 24 hours. Just before serving, stir in parsley and basil. Serve on lettuce leaves.

Standard oven: Preheat to 450°F; roast about 30 minutes.

TARRAGON ROASTED CORN ○

An easy way to cook fresh corn with a tarragon tang.

Serves 4
4 ears of sweet corn
2 tablespoons melted butter or margarine
1/2 teaspoon dried tarragon, crushed
Salt
Freshly ground black pepper

Bakeware: Four 8 × 12-inch pieces of aluminum foil; 1 oven rack with drip pan in place

Preheat convection oven to 350°F. Stack the 4 sheets of aluminum foil and place 1 ear of corn on top. Brush ear generously with melted butter and sprinkle with 1/8 teaspoon crushed tarragon, salt and pepper. Wrap ear in top sheet of aluminum foil. Repeat with remaining 3 ears of corn and place ears on oven rack leaving at least 1 inch of space between ears. Slide rack into preheated oven and roast 15 to 20 minutes or until kernels are tender. Brush with additional butter, if desired.

Standard oven: Preheat to 400°F; roast corn on oven rack 15 to 20 minutes or until kernels are tender.

convection and standard broiling

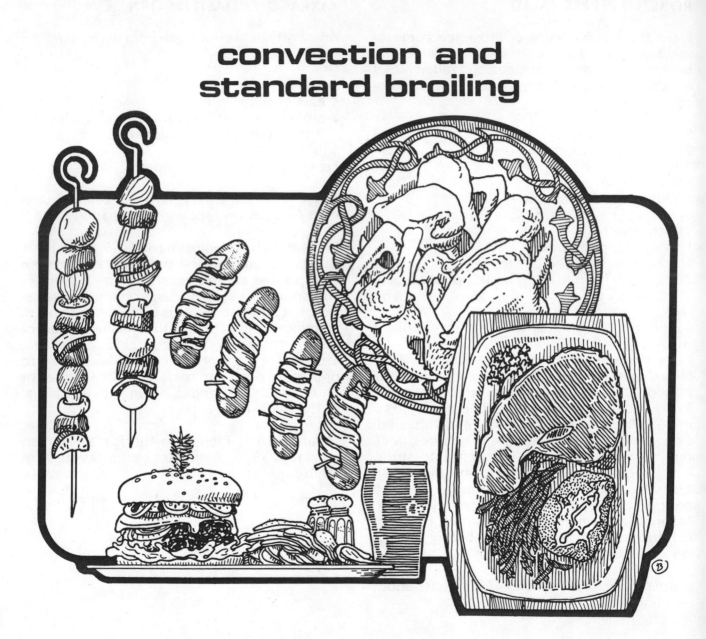

BROILING

Broiling, the most primitive of all cooking techniques, is becoming more and more popular today. Cooking foods quickly with direct, high heat seems to fit beautifully and appropriately into our hectic life styles. The growth in popularity of steakhouses and restaurant-grills attests to the fact that broiled meats hold the interest of modern man just as that first chunk of meat cooked on a stick over an open fire fascinated the first caveman.

Broiling has many advantages that we of the busy modern-day schedules can appreciate. It is fast, produces delicious and comparatively low-calorie dishes and is relatively easy to do. Convection broiling is all this with slightly different results.

HOW STANDARD BROILING AND CONVECTION BROILING DIFFER

There are differences in both technique and results when comparing standard and convection broiling:

● Standard-broiled foods must be cooked at the proper distance from the heat source for the proper length of time. This can vary greatly depending upon the type and thickness of food and the desired degree of doneness. With convection broiling, you don't have to worry about the distance of the food from the heat—the heat is all around. Food is placed directly on the oven rack in the middle of the oven and is cooked by circulating hot air so that the distance from the heat source does not have to be calculated.

● Standard broiling cooks foods on one side at a time and foods must be turned over halfway through cooking time. Convection-broiled foods need not be turned since they are cooked from both sides at once.

Note: With top-fan ovens, the tops of foods may brown faster than the bottoms. Check halfway through cooking and if the difference bothers you, do turn over the foods. Side-fan ovens may cause edges—especially those near the fan—to brown faster than tops and bottoms. If an *over-browning spot* bothers you, shift the position of the item during cooking.,

● Standard-broiled foods have a crusty exterior; convection-broiled foods have a more tender exterior. Individuals who like their steaks broiled to a crusty, well-browned exterior may not like convection-broiled steaks. However, the more delicate broiling of convection does a superior job with those items that tend to dry out when standard-broiled, such as chicken, fish and pork chops.

● Convection-broiled meats tend to shrink less than standard-broiled meats. The searing action of the circulating hot air seals in the juices and gives a juicier, more plump product.

● Standard-broiled and convection-broiled foods cook in about the same amount of time. Convection-broiled foods don't have to be turned during broiling.

FOODS FOR CONVECTION BROILING

Those foods you are used to standard broiling can be convection broiled. Tender cuts of meat and poultry are best for broiling of any sort. Steaks, hamburgers, chicken pieces and quarters, lamb chops, pork chops, whole fish, fish steaks and fillets, hot dogs and sausages can all be convection broiled with delicious results. Fruits and vegetables can also be broiled successfully.

Sausage is one food we often forget when thinking about broiling and that's really a shame. It could be because most of us were raised on the pre-packaged cellophane-covered varieties of supermarket sausages. I was fortunate to grow up in an area that offered no less than six independently owned and operated butcher shops within 15 minutes of home. Each butcher had his own recipe for his very special home-made sausages and took pride in the way he combined just the right proportion of meat, fat and spices to get exactly the right flavor that was distinctly his own. If you have ever walked into a butcher shop on a Saturday morning and smelled the aroma of fresh and smoked sausages, you would never again think of sausage in the same way. And you would never again be totally satisfied with those supermarket versions.

If you can find an ethnic neighborhood where small businesses still thrive, you will probably find the most interesting and delicious sausages you have ever tasted. Italian sausage, Polish sausage, *klobasy, jaternice, chorizos* and many others are good selections for convection broiling. So explore butcher shops for sausages with character that will expand your broiling repertoire. See pages 95 and 96 for sausage recipes.

MARINADES AND BASTING SAUCES

A marinade will add flavor to meat and other broiler foods, but don't expect it to tenderize a tough cut. Broiler meats should be tender cuts. If you wish to broil a less tender cut, use meat tenderizer according to package directions. This is not a bad idea, since what less tender cuts lack in tenderness they make up for in flavor.

A basting sauce can be brushed on food just before broiling to add flavor and to aid in browning. A basic basting sauce of melted butter or margarine, freshly ground pepper and seasoned salt is especially nice on chicken, pork chops, lamb chops and fish, and can even be used on 3/4- to 1-inch-thick steaks to aid in browning since they cook quickly.

BROILING FROZEN MEATS

Frozen broiler cuts of meat and poultry can be broiled successfully in a convection oven. This is not only a time-saving technique but one that does not sacrifice quality. There is no appreciable difference between frozen broiled meats and fresh broiled meats as long as this simple procedure is followed:

● Select cuts one to two inches thick for best results. Thinner cuts may not look brown on the outside when done throughout, and thicker cuts might be over-browned on the outside while still undercooked in the center.

● Season frozen meat and poultry by brushing all surfaces with a basting sauce made of oil, melted butter or margarine, salt or seasoned salt, pepper and any other spices you desire.

The basting sauce will solidify on the frozen food and begin to lend its flavors to the food as soon as it begins to melt in the oven. Because broiling time is much shorter than roasting time, this method is preferable to the roasting method of seasoning halfway through cooking time.

● Increase broiling time by five to 10 minutes. If the frozen item is placed in a cold oven, increase broiling time by an additional 10 to 20 minutes.

● To test doneness, insert an instant-read thermometer in edge of steak or chop or in meaty part of poultry pieces about five minutes before estimated broiling time is up.

KABOBS—AN INTERNATIONAL FAVORITE

In Turkey they're called *shish kebab,* in France *en brochette,* in Russia *shashlik* and in Indonesia *sate.* Here in the States we call them kabobs.

No matter what you call them, kabobs are a wonderful way to serve meat, vegetables or meat and vegetables in combination. One of the advantages of serving kabobs is in stretching your meat dollar. While 1-1/2 pounds of steak may serve 2 to 3 people, 1-1/2 pounds of steak cut into chunks for kabobs can serve 4 to 6 people when skewered with chunks of vegetables. Kabobs are especially well-suited to convection cooking as the skewers do not have to be turned for even browning—this happens automatically due to the forced air flow.

Many different meats can be used for kabob cookery: beef, pork, lamb, chicken, even ground meat (see Turkish Ground Beef Kabobs, page 98). Seafood, including scallops, shrimp and lobster, may be used for kabobs but must be basted well to keep from drying out during cooking. Meats for kabob cooking should be tender cuts and are often marinated to impart a particular flavor and to add oil to very lean cuts. Remember these hints when cooking kabobs and see pages 98, 99, 106 and 108 for recipes:

● Select skewers that will fit in your oven without touching the oven walls. Skewers 10 to 11 inches long will fit most convection ovens.

● Cut foods into uniform pieces for even cooking.

● Combine foods that will cook in the same amount of time. Often fresh vegetables have to be blanched (cooked in boiling water) for a few minutes to give them a head start on the meat since some vegetables, such as zucchini, onions and green peppers, take longer to cook than meat, especially if the meat is cooked to rare. If you don't wish to take this extra blanching step, thread meat and vegetables on separate skewers and start cooking the vegetable skewers before the meat skewers so they can be removed from the oven and served at the same time.

● For rare meat, push items close together on skewer. For meat that is well done and slightly crustier, leave a small amount of space between items on skewer.

BROILING CLEANUP

One question that always comes up when the topic is broiling is "Will it be hard to clean the oven after broiling?" All broiling is somewhat messy; it is the nature of the technique to spatter since intense high heat is applied to an item that contains fat.

Convection broiling cleanup is not difficult unless the messiness is allowed to build up. Always clean your oven after broiling. In most units, the oven walls are made of a continuous-clean material that will convert spatters to a fine powder during normal use. The walls and floor of the oven can be wiped with a damp sponge. The oven rack and drip pan can be washed in hot soapy water or in the dishwasher. (See your oven's care-and-use manual for specific directions.) For easier cleaning, soak rack and drip pan in hot, soapy water before washing. The door can be washed in hot soapy water if it is immersible (check care-and-use manual for dishwasher directions) or with a glass cleaner and a soft cloth if not immersible.

CONVECTION BROILING GUIDELINES

● **Select Broiler Meats by Thickness.** Thickness is more important in broiling than weight. Select thick cuts for rare-meat lovers and thin cuts for fans of well-done meat if you wish them to cook in the same time.
● **Always Have Drip Pan in Place.**
● **Set the Temperature Control at the "Broil" Setting Recommended in Your Convection Oven's Care-and-Use Manual.** "Broil" temperatures vary from oven to oven but all fall within the 400° to 475°F range. Recipes for delicate items such as fruits and seafood may call for a lower temperature.

● **Preheat the Oven According to Manufacturer's Directions.** If the manufacturer does not recommend a preheating time and you wish to preheat, 10 to 15 minutes is sufficient. See pages 12-14 for the "whys" of preheating.
● **The Oven Rack (Broiler Rack) Can Be Left in the Oven or Removed During Preheating.** See care-and-use manual for the recommendation on your oven. The advantage of leaving the oven rack in the oven during preheating is that broiler foods placed on it begin to cook and sear as soon as they make contact with the rack. This works best when only one or two items are broiled. If there are several items, such as parts of a cut-up chicken, it is best to place them on a cool rack and slide the rack into the center of the preheated oven. The important factor is the length of time the oven door is open. If open too long, the oven temperature drops too much for efficient broiling.
● **Remove Food with Tongs.** When broiling time is up, slide rack out of oven and use tongs to remove items to serving plates. Do not puncture meats with a fork or natural juices will be lost.

- **Place a Small Jelly Roll Pan on the Counter in Front of the Oven.** This helps keep the counter-top clean by catching drips that may fall from the rack as it is removed.
- **Broiler Meats Do Not Need to Rest After Cooking.** Use an instant-read thermometer (page 71) inserted into the edge of the meat to test the degree of doneness of thick steaks and chops. Look for the following internal temperatures when broiling.

TEMPERATURES FOR BROILED MEATS

Beef (steaks, kabobs and patties)
Rare	140°F
Medium	160°F
Well done	170°F

Pork (chops, kabobs and patties)
Medium well	160°F

Lamb (chops, steaks and kabobs)
Rare	140°F
Medium	160°F
Well done	170°F

- **Brush Broiler Foods with Barbecue Sauce or Glaze During the Last Five Minutes of Broiling.** Earlier brushing may cause scorching, especially if the sauce contains sugar.
- **Cook Broiler Foods on One Rack.** If foods are broiled on two racks, drippings from the top rack will drain onto bottom rack foods; this may not be desirable and also may increase cooking time. Broil on a rack placed in the center or lower portion of the oven. Other foods that cook at the same temperature as the "Broil" setting can be cooked on the top rack as long as one inch of air space surrounds all items.

LUNCHEON AND SUPPER DISHES AND KABOBS

PIGS IN BLANKETS (Franks in Bacon) ○

This simple lunch dish can be made in any quantity as long as you leave at least 1 inch of space between sausages.

Serves 4
4 slices bacon
4 frankfurters, bratwursts or other ethnic sausages
4 French or Italian rolls or hot dog buns

Bakeware: 1 oven rack with drip pan in place

Preheat convection oven to 400°F. Wrap bacon slice around each frank in spiral fashion; fasten ends of bacon to frank with toothpicks. Place on oven rack, slide into center of preheated oven and broil about 10 minutes or until frank is brown and bacon is crisp. Serve with rolls. Garnish with your favorite condiments.

Standard oven: Preheat 5 to 10 minutes at "Broil"; broil 4 to 5 inches from heat source, 5 minutes per side.

ENGLISH MUFFIN PIZZAS

Great for brunch or lunch.

Serves 4
1/2 pound sweet or hot Italian sausage
2/3 cup Pizza Sauce, page 133
1/4 teaspoon dried oregano, crushed
1 tablespoon minced onion
4 English muffins, split and toasted
1 cup shredded mozzarella cheese

Bakeware: 1 or 2 oven racks with drip pan in place

Preheat convection oven at "Broil" according to oven directions. Remove sausage meat from casings and brown in skillet over medium heat. Pour off excess fat and stir in pizza sauce, oregano and minced onion. Heat to boiling. Place English muffins on oven rack(s), toasted side up. Spoon pizza sauce mixture onto muffins and top with cheese. Slide rack into center of oven and broil until mixture bubbles and cheese melts, about 5 minutes.

Standard oven: Preheat 5 to 10 minutes at "Broil"; broil 4 to 5 inches from heat source until sauce is bubbly and cheese is melted, about 5 minutes.

BROILED CHORIZO TACOS

Chorizos can be found in Mexican groceries and some specialty shops. They are spicy little sausages with a distinctive flavor.

Serves 4
1 large avocado
2 to 3 teaspoons lemon juice
Pinch salt
Pinch chili powder
2 ripe tomatoes, peeled, seeded and chopped
1 small onion, peeled and chopped
1 teaspoon minced fresh coriander (cilantro) or parsley
8 small *chorizos* (Mexican pork sausages)
8 corn tortillas, heated on a dry frypan

Bakeware: 1 oven rack with drip pan in place

Peel avocado, remove pit and mash meat with fork. Stir in lemon juice, salt and chili powder. Set aside. Combine tomato, onion and fresh coriander and set aside. Preheat convection oven at "Broil" according to oven directions. Prick *chorizos* and place on oven rack, leaving at least 1 inch of space between sausages, and slide rack into preheated oven. Broil 15 to 20 minutes or until sausages are brown. Remove casings and crumble meat. To assemble tacos, spoon avocado mixture onto warm tortillas and top with crumbled meat and tomato-onion mixture. Fold in half to eat.

Standard oven: Preheat 5 to 10 minutes at "Broil"; broil *chorizos* 4 to 5 inches from heat 15 to 20 minutes, turning *chorizos* over halfway through cooking time.

BROILED HAMBURGERS WITH ONION

For the onion-lovers in your family.

Serves 4
1 pound ground beef
1/4 cup finely chopped sweet green pepper
1 teaspoon Seasoned Salt, page 138
1/4 teaspoon freshly ground pepper
4 large onion slices, each 1/4 inch thick
Bacon drippings or melted margarine
4 hamburger buns

Bakeware: 1 oven rack with drip pan in place

Preheat convection oven at "Broil" according to oven directions. Mix together ground beef, green pepper, seasoned salt and pepper. Shape into four 1/2-inch-thick patties. Set aside. Brush both sides of onion slices with bacon drippings. Place on oven rack leaving at least 1 inch space between slices. Slide rack into center of preheated oven and broil 5 to 7 minutes or until slightly undercooked for your taste. Top each slice with a hamburger patty, return to oven and broil 10 minutes for rare, 12 minutes for medium or 15 minutes for well done. Serve on hamburger buns.

Standard oven: Preheat 5 to 10 minutes at "Broil"; broil onion slices about 5 minutes, turning slices halfway through cooking time; add patties and broil as directed for Mushroom Burgers, following, turning patties halfway through cooking time.

MUSHROOM BURGERS O

A change-of-pace burger that can be served on a bun for lunch or as an entrée for dinner.

Serves 4
1/4 pound mushrooms, chopped
1 pound ground beef
2 tablespoons minced onion
1 teaspoon salt
1 tablespoon Worcestershire sauce
1/8 teaspoon freshly ground pepper

Bakeware: 1 oven rack with drip pan in place

Preheat convection oven at "Broil" according to oven directions. Mix together all ingredients and shape into four 1/2-inch-thick patties. Place on oven rack. Slide rack into center of oven and broil 10 minutes for rare, 12 minutes for medium and 15 minutes for well done.

Standard oven: Preheat 5 to 10 minutes at "Broil"; broil 3 inches from heat source 3 minutes per side for rare, 4 to 5 minutes per side for medium and 6 to 7 minutes per side for well done.

TURKISH GROUND BEEF KABOBS

A change-of-pace entrée of ground beef kabobs served over pita bread with a tangy yogurt sauce. If you don't have a mint plant growing in your yard, this recipe is a good reason to start one. These perennials grow very easily and will give you a steady supply of leaves during the summer.

Serves 4 to 6

YOGURT SAUCE
1-1/2 cups unflavored yogurt
1/4 cup minced parsley
1 tablespoon minced mint, or 1/2 tablespoon dried mint
1 tablespoon minced chives, or 1/2 tablespoon dried chives
1/2 teaspooon salt
1/2 cup diced peeled and seeded cucumber

MEATBALL KABOBS
1-1/2 pounds ground beef
3/4 cup cooked rice, cooled
1/4 cup minced onion
1-1/2 tablespoons minced mint, or 1/2 tablespoon dried mint
1-1/2 tablespoons minced parsley
2 teaspoons salt
1/4 teaspoon ground allspice
1/4 teaspoon ground cinnamon
1/4 teaspoon freshly ground pepper
2 medium zucchini, peeled and cut into 1/2-inch slices

BASTING SAUCE
3 tablespoons olive oil
2 tablespoons lemon juice
1 tablespoon minced mint, or 1/2 tablespoon dried mint

4 pita breads
1 cup chopped tomatoes

Bakeware: 1 oven rack with drip pan in place; four 12-inch metal skewers or skewers to fit your oven

Preheat convection oven at "Broil" according to oven directions. Stir together all yogurt sauce ingredients; set aside at room temperature. Mix together all meatball kabob ingredients except zucchini and form into 16 meatballs. Thread 4 meatballs on each skewer, alternating with zucchini slices.

Mix together basting sauce ingredients. Brush over meat and zucchini on skewers. Place skewers on oven rack spaced at least 1 inch apart. Slide rack into center of preheated oven and broil about 10 minutes. While kabobs are cooking, heat pita bread in standard oven according to package directions. To serve, cut pita breads into fourths, arrange on serving platter and top with a few spoonfuls of yogurt sauce. Place meat and zucchini on bread and top with more sauce and chopped tomato. Pass remaining yogurt sauce in sauceboat.

Standard oven: Preheat 5 to 10 minutes at "Broil"; broil kabobs 4 inches from heat source about 10 minutes, turning and basting once.

BROILED SCALLOP KABOBS O

An entrée that's easy and attractive.

Serves 4
4 tablespoons (1/2 stick) butter or margarine, melted
2 tablespoons lemon juice
2 garlic cloves, crushed
1/2 teaspoon Worcestershire sauce
1/2 teaspoon salt
1/8 teaspoon dried thyme, finely crushed
1 pound fresh or frozen scallops
1 jar (4 ounces) whole pimiento, cut into 1-inch pieces
Lemon wedges

Bakeware: 1 oven rack with drip pan in place; 4 skewers to fit oven

Preheat convection oven at "Broil" according to oven directions. Stir together melted butter, lemon juice, garlic, Worcestershire sauce, salt and thyme. Thread scallops and pimiento pieces alternately on wooden skewers. Brush each kabob generously on all sides with melted butter mixture. Place kabobs on oven rack, leaving 1 inch of air space all around. Slide rack into center of preheated oven and broil 5 to 8 minutes or until scallops have turned opaque. Baste once with butter sauce during broiling. Serve with lemon wedges and use remaining butter sauce for dipping, if desired. (Be careful not to overcook scallops or they will toughen.)

Standard oven: Preheat 5 to 10 minutes at "Broil"; place kabobs on broiler pan and broil 4 inches from heat for 6 to 10 minutes or until scallops are opaque, turning and basting once.

MEAT, CHICKEN AND FISH

BROILED BREADED PORK CHOPS O

This technique could be called "frying" in a convection oven, because the breading becomes crisp, as if fried.

Serves 4
1 cup dried bread crumbs
1/4 cup grated Parmesan cheese
1 teaspoon Seasoned Salt, page 138
1/8 teaspoon freshly ground pepper
4 pork chops, 3/4 to 1 inch thick
Olive oil

Bakeware: 1 oven rack with drip pan in place

Preheat convection oven at "Broil" according to oven directions. Stir together crumbs, cheese, salt and pepper. Brush pork chops with olive oil on both sides and all edges. Coat with bread crumb mixture, gently pressing crumbs in place. Place chops on oven rack, slide into center of preheated oven and broil 20 to 25 minutes or until crumbs are golden brown.

Standard oven: Preheat 5 to 10 minutes at "Broil"; broil chops about 5 inches from heat 10 to 15 minutes per side or until crumbs are golden brown.

HERBED BROILED PORK CHOPS ○

Setting the convection oven at 425°F allows the delicate broiling needed for keeping pork chops juicy and succulent while cooking them thoroughly.

Serves 4 to 6
6 rib or loin pork chops, about 1 inch thick
1 tablespoon Herbes de Provence, page 137
1/2 teaspoon salt
Freshly ground black pepper

Bakeware: 1 oven rack with drip pan in place

Preheat convection oven to 425°F. Slash fat along pork chop edges at 1/2-inch intervals. Mix Herbes de Provence with salt and ground pepper and press to both sides of each chop. Let stand about 15 minutes. Place on oven rack, slide into center of preheated oven and broil 15 to 20 minutes or until chops are brown.

Standard oven: Preheat 5 to 10 minutes at "Broil"; broil chops 4 to 5 inches from heat source for 15 to 20 minutes, turning chops halfway through cooking time.

HAM SLICE WITH PLUM SAUCE

An easy dish made with an economical cut of meat.

Serves 4 to 6
1/2 cup plum jelly
2 tablespoons water
1-1/2 teaspoons red wine vinegar
1 tablespoon chili sauce
Pinch ground ginger
1 teaspoon cornstarch
1 tablespoon water
2 ham slices, each 1 inch thick (a total of
    1-1/2 to 2 pounds)

Bakeware: 1 oven rack with drip pan in place

Preheat convection oven at "Broil" according to oven directions. Heat plum jelly, 2 tablespoons water, vinegar, chili sauce and ginger in small saucepan over medium heat until jelly melts. Stir cornstarch into 1 tablespoon water, whisk into jelly mixture and heat to boiling, stirring constantly. Boil 2 minutes, stirring constantly. Remove from heat. Place ham slices on oven rack, baste with sauce, slide rack into center of preheated oven and broil 15 to 20 minutes, basting with plum sauce every 5 minutes. Serve warm sauce in gravyboat with ham.

Standard oven: Preheat 5 to 10 minutes at "Broil"; broil about 5 inches from heat source 15 to 20 minutes, turning slices over halfway through cooking time.

MEDITERRANEAN-STYLE BROILED LAMB CHOPS ☆

An herb coating of Mediterranean flavorings turns lamb chops into gourmet fare.

Serves 4 to 6
6 rib or loin lamb chops, about 1-1/2
   inches thick
1 large garlic clove, peeled and cut into 6 slivers
1-1/2 teaspoons salt
1/2 teaspoon freshly ground black pepper
1 teaspoon ground sage
1 teaspoon dried oregano, crushed
1/8 teaspoon ground cumin

Bakeware: 1 oven rack with drip pan in place

Preheat convection oven at "Broil" according to oven directions. Slash fat along lamb chop edges at 1/2-inch intervals. Use point of paring knife to make a narrow deep slit in center of each chop; insert one garlic sliver in each slit. Stir together salt, pepper, sage, oregano and cumin and rub onto both sides and edges of chops. Place chops on oven rack and slide rack into center of preheated oven. Broil 15 to 17 minutes for rare, 20 to 22 minutes for medium and 25 to 27 minutes for well done.

Standard oven: Preheat 5 to 10 minutes at "Broil"; broil 4 to 5 inches from heat source according to times listed above, turning chops once halfway through cooking time.

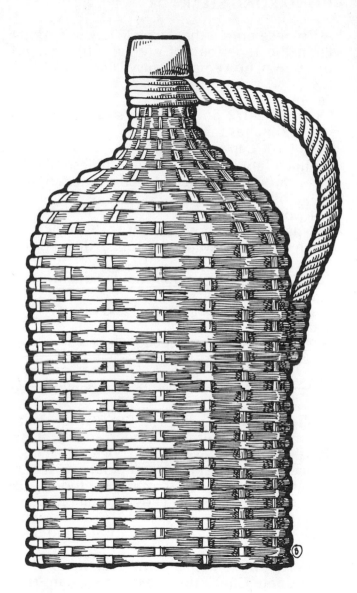

HONG KONG STEAK ☆

A Chinese entrée that steak-lovers will adore! From the repertoire of my good friends and teachers, Chu Yen and Pansy Luke.

Serves 4 to 6
One 2- to 2-1/2-pound sirloin steak, about 1-1/2 inches thick
About 1/4 cup hoisin sauce
1 ounce (about 1 cup) whole Chinese black mushrooms,* soaked in warm water about 1/2 hour
1/4 pound snow peas*
1/2 pound bok choy,* cut into 1-inch dice
1 can (8 ounces) water chestnuts,* drained and sliced
1 can (8 ounces) bamboo shoots,* drained and sliced
1 sweet red pepper, seeded and diced
1 tablespoon peanut oil
About 1/4 cup oyster sauce*, at room temperature

Bakeware: 1 oven rack with drip pan in place

Preheat convection oven at "Broil" according to oven directions. Slash fat around edge of steak. Brush steak on both sides and edges with hoisin sauce. Let stand at room temperature 10 minutes. Trim stems from soaked mushrooms; discard. Cut mushroom caps in half. Remove stems from snow peas. Place steak on oven rack, slide rack into center of preheated oven and broil 10 to 12 minutes for rare, 14 to 16 minutes for medium and 18 to 20 minutes for well done. Check doneness with instant-read thermometer inserted in edge of steak.

While steak is broiling, stir-fry vegetables: Heat peanut oil in wok or large skillet. Add bok choy, water chestnuts, bamboo shoots, mushrooms, snow peas and pepper, in that order, stir-frying over high heat until vegetables are crisp-tender, about 5 minutes. To serve, place hot vegetables on serving platter and top with broiled steak. Working quickly, cut steak diagonally into serving-sized strips about 2 inches wide. Pour oyster sauce evenly over steak. Serve immediately with steamed rice.

Standard oven: Preheat 5 to 10 minutes at "Broil"; broil according to times listed above, turning steak halfway through cooking time.

*Available at Oriental food markets or in Chinese sections of some supermarkets.

BASICALLY DELICIOUS CHICKEN

So simple and so good; this will become a family favorite.

Serves 4
1 cut-up chicken, about 2-1/2 pounds
4 to 6 tablespoons melted butter or margarine
1/4 teaspoon Seasoned Salt, page 138
Freshly ground pepper

Bakeware: 1 oven rack with drip pan in place

For crisply broiled chicken, preheat convection oven at "Broil" according to oven directions; for delicately broiled chicken, preheat at 400°F. Pat chicken pieces dry with paper toweling. Stir seasoned salt and pepper into melted butter. Brush chicken pieces on all sides with butter mixture. Place on oven rack and slide into preheated oven. Broil white meat 20 to 25 minutes, dark meat 25 to 30 minutes. If chicken drippings create smoking during broiling, pour a few tablespoons of water into drip pan in bottom of oven.

Standard oven: Preheat 5 to 10 minutes at "Broil"; broil 5 to 6 inches from heat source for about 30 minutes, turning chicken halfway through cooking time.

PROVENÇAL BROILED CHICKEN

The flavors of sunny Southern France enhance the versatile chicken.

Serves 4
1 broiler-fryer, quartered (about 3 to 3-1/2
    pounds)
Melted butter or margarine
Salt
Freshly ground pepper
1 to 2 tablespoons olive oil
1 medium onion, halved and sliced
1 medium sweet green pepper, seeded and
    cut into 1/4-inch strips
1 medium red sweet pepper, seeded and cut
    into 1/4-inch strips
2 garlic cloves, crushed
1/4 teaspoon Herbes de Provence, page 137
1/2 teaspoon salt
Freshly ground pepper to taste
1/4 cup French- or Italian-style black olives

Bakeware: 1 oven rack with drip pan in place

Preheat convection oven at "Broil" according to oven directions. Brush both sides of chicken quarters with melted butter and sprinkle with salt and pepper. Place on convection oven rack skin side up, leaving at least 1 inch of air space between the quarters. Broil 15 to 20 minutes, basting with additional butter, if desired. While chicken is cooking, make pepper mixture: Heat olive oil over medium heat in 10-inch skillet. Add onion and green and red pepper strips; stir for 1 minute. Add garlic, Herbes de Provence and 1/2 teaspoon salt and pepper; cook and stir until peppers are slightly cooked; stir in olives. After chicken has cooked 15 to 20 minutes, push quarters together on rack and spoon pepper mixture over chicken. Return to oven for 5 minutes.

Standard oven: Preheat 5 to 10 minutes at "Broil"; broil 5 inches from heat source about 25 minutes, turning chicken over halfway through cooking time. After adding pepper mixture, return to broiler 3 to 5 minutes; watch carefully to prevent burning.

BROILED SALMON STEAKS CHINOISE ○

A tangy marinade gives Oriental inspiration to salmon.

Serves 4
4 salmon steaks, about 6 ounces each

MARINADE
1/4 cup orange or pineapple juice
1/4 cup soy sauce
1 tablespoon peanut oil
1 tablespoon catsup
2 tablespoons minced fresh coriander or
  parsley
1 tablespoon lemon juice
1 garlic clove, crushed
1/2 teaspoon aniseed, crushed

Salt
1/4 teaspoon freshly ground black pepper

Bakeware: 1 oven rack with drip pan in place

Place salmon steaks in single layer in shallow glass dish. Combine orange juice, soy sauce, peanut oil, catsup, coriander, lemon juice, garlic and aniseed and pour over salmon steaks. Turn over each steak to coat with marinade and cover and refrigerate 30 to 40 minutes, turning 2 to 3 times. Preheat convection oven to 425°F. Remove steaks from marinade, salt and pepper lightly on both sides and place on oven rack leaving at least 1 inch of space between steaks. Slide into center of preheated oven and broil 10 to 15 minutes, basting 2 or 3 times with marinade. Salmon is done when the meat flakes but is still moist. While salmon is broiling, pour marinade into saucepan, bring to a boil and boil 5 minutes. Spoon a small amount of hot marinade over each salmon steak when served.

Standard oven: Preheat 5 to 10 minutes at "Broil"; broil 5 inches from heat 6 to 8 minutes per side.

BROILED KING CRAB LEGS ○

This special treat doesn't have to be reserved for restaurant fare. Try it in your convection oven!

Serves 4
About 1-1/2 pounds frozen split Alaska king crab legs, thawed
1/4 cup melted butter or margarine
1 tablespoons lemon juice
1 teaspoon grated onion
1/4 teaspoon Seasoned Salt, page 138, or salt
1/2 teaspoon dried tarragon, crushed

Bakeware: 1 oven rack with drip pan in place

Preheat convection oven at "Broil." Place thawed crab legs on oven rack, meaty side up, leaving space between legs. Combine remaining ingredients and brush onto crab meat. Slide oven rack into center of preheated oven and broil about 5 minutes, basting with butter mixture once or twice. Serve warm butter mixture as dipping sauce with crab.

Standard oven: Preheat 5 to 10 minutes at "Broil"; broil crab legs meaty side up 4 to 5 inches from heat source about 5 minutes.

VEGETABLES, APPETIZERS AND DESSERTS

COTTAGE FRIES

Leave the potato skins on for added flavor and nutrition.

Serves 4
4 tablespoons butter or margarine, melted
4 medium potatoes, scrubbed and sliced 1/8 inch thick
Salt
Freshly ground pepper

Bakeware: 1 or 2 aluminum jelly roll pans to fit oven

Preheat convection oven at "Broil" according to oven directions. Brush jelly roll pan(s) lightly with melted butter, reserving remaining butter. Place potato slices on jelly roll pan in single layer. Brush with remaining melted butter and sprinkle with salt and pepper. Broil 15 to 25 minutes depending upon desired brownness. Serve immediately.

Standard oven: Preheat 5 to 10 minutes at "Broil"; broil 5 to 6 inches from heat source 15 to 25 minutes.

SAGANAKI ☆

A dramatic Greek appetizer! Have all ingredients ready so the flaming goes quickly and smoothly.

Serves 4
1/2 pound *kefalotiri* cheese, about
   1/2 inch thick
1 tablespoon melted butter or margarine
1 teaspoon lemon juice
1 tablespoon brandy
1/2 lemon
4 lemon wedges

Bakeware: 1 shallow flameproof casserole or skillet (flameproof ceramic is good)

Preheat convection oven at "Broil" according to oven directions. Cut cheese into 4 wedges; place in flameproof casserole so at least 1 inch of space surrounds each wedge. Mix together melted butter and 1 teaspoon lemon juice. Brush cheese with lemon butter. Place in preheated oven and broil about 5 minutes or until cheese is bubbly and light brown. Now you must work quickly to produce a dramatic effect: Remove cheese from oven and place on flameproof tray or surface. If moving cheese into another room to flame, have brandy, lemon half and matches on tray ready to go. While cheese is still hot and sizzling, pour brandy over cheese and ignite with match. Squeeze lemon half over cheese as flames die down. Using spatula or pancake turner, remove cheese to warm serving plates and garnish each plate with a lemon wedge.

Standard oven: Preheat 5 to 10 minutes at "Broil"; broil cheese 4 to 6 inches from heat source until bubbly and light brown.

BACON-WRAPPED SHRIMP EN BROCHETTE

Shrimp combine with bacon and blue cheese to make the perfect cocktail appetizer for a special dinner party.

Makes 12 appetizer servings (2 shrimp each)
12 bacon slices, cut in half crosswise
About 1/4 pound blue cheese, at room
   temperature
Freshly ground black pepper
24 medium shrimp (about 1 pound), shelled
   deveined
12 small lemon wedges

Bakeware: 1 aluminum foil broiler pan or microwave paper broiler pan to fit oven; 12 metal or bamboo skewers, 5 to 6 inches long; 1 oven rack with drip pan in place

Preheat convection oven to 400°F. Place bacon pieces in single layer in broiler pan, slide pan into preheated oven and cook 5 to 10 minutes or until bacon turns light brown and is still pliable. Remove from pan and cool to handling temperature. Beat cheese in small bowl until smooth. Sprinkle bacon strips lightly with pepper and spread cheese evenly on peppered side of each strip. Beginning at narrow end, wrap bacon around shrimp and thread 2 wrapped shrimp on each skewer. (Shrimp can be completed to this point up to 12 hours before serving; wrap and refrigerate.) Preheat convection oven at "Broil" according to oven directions. Place skewers on oven rack, slide rack into center of preheated oven and broil 5 to 10 minutes or until shrimp are opaque and bacon is crisp. Remove from oven, thread one lemon wedge on the end of each skewer and line up on serving platter.

Standard oven: Bake bacon in aluminum foil broiler pan or skillet as described above. Preheat oven 5 to 10 minutes at "Broil"; broil shrimp about 5 inches from heat for about 15 minutes, turning shrimp over halfway through cooking time.

STUFFED MUSHROOMS

Pass these savory tidbits at cocktail time.

Makes 24
24 large mushrooms (about 1-1/2 pounds)
1 garlic clove, crushed
3 tablespoons butter or margarine
6 ounces bulk pork sausage
6 tablespoons dried bread crumbs
6 tablespoons grated Parmesan cheese
4 tablespoons minced parsley
Seasoned Salt, page 108
Freshly ground black pepper
Melted butter or margarine

Bakeware: 1 or 2 aluminum baking sheets to fit oven.

Pull stems from mushrooms and chop; reserve caps. Cook chopped mushrooms and garlic in butter over medium heat until mushrooms are soft, about 3 minutes. Add sausage and cook and stir until sausage is brown. Stir in bread crumbs, cheese and parsley. Taste and season with seasoned salt and pepper. Using a teaspoon, fill mushroom caps with sausage mixture, place caps on baking sheet(s) and brush each cap with melted butter. Preheat convection oven at "Broil" with oven rack(s) in place. Slide baking sheet(s) into center of oven and broil 3 to 5 minutes or until brown and bubbly.

Standard oven: Preheat 5 to 10 minutes at "Broil"; broil about 4 inches from heat source 3 to 5 minutes.

YAKITORI

Since skinned and boned chicken breasts contain no fat, this appetizer can be broiled on two racks if needed.

Serves 4 to 6 as an appetizer

MARINADE
1/2 cup soy sauce
1/4 cup Japanese sweet rice cooking wine or sherry
1 teaspoon minced ginger root
1/2 tablespoon honey

3 whole skinned boned chicken breasts
6 to 8 green onions, white portion only
Peanut oil

Bakeware: Four to six 5- to 6-inch wooden picks; 1 oven rack with drip pan in place

Stir together soy sauce, wine, ginger root and honey in small saucepan. Bring to a boil, simmer 1 minute and cool to room temperature. Cut chicken breasts and onions into 1-inch pieces; place in shallow glass dish and pour cooled marinade over the pieces. Allow pieces to marinate 15 minutes. Preheat convection oven at "Broil." Thread wooden picks alternately with chicken and onion pieces. Brush lightly with peanut oil and place picks on 1 or 2 oven racks, leaving at least 1 inch of space between skewers. Slide rack into preheated oven and broil 8 to 10 minutes.

Standard oven: Preheat 5 to 10 minutes at "Broil"; broil skewers 3 to 4 inches from heat source about 5 minutes per side.

BROILED BANANAS O

If you prepare the butter mixture ahead of time, this fruity dessert goes together very quickly.

Serves 4
Soft butter or margarine
4 barely ripe bananas
1 tablespoon lime or lemon juice
4 tablespoons (1/2 stick) butter, softened
1/4 cup packed brown sugar
1/4 teaspoon ground cinnamon
1/8 teaspoon freshly grated nutmeg
1/2 tablespoon dark rum (optional)
2 tablespoons golden raisins
2 tablespoons chopped almonds or walnuts

Bakeware: 1 aluminum or aluminum foil jelly roll pan to fit oven

Preheat convection oven 5 minutes at "Broil." Generously butter pan. Peel bananas and cut in half crosswise. Place in pan 1 inch apart and brush with lime juice, reserving remaining juice. Mix together 4 tablespoons soft butter, brown sugar, cinnamon, nutmeg and optional rum. Spread mixture over bananas. Broil in center of preheated oven 3 to 4 minutes. Sprinkle with remaining lime juice, remove to dessert dishes and top with raisins and nuts.

Standard oven: Preheat 5 to 10 minutes at "Broil"; broil 3 to 4 minutes about 4 inches from heat source.

ICE CREAM-TOPPED BANANAS Place 2 broiled banana pieces on dessert dish, top with scoop of vanilla ice cream and sprinkle with raisins and nuts.

BROILED APRICOTS O

A nice garnish for roasted pork and poultry.

Makes 8 apricot halves
1 tablespoon butter or margarine, softened
2 tablespoons packed brown sugar
1/4 teaspoon ground cinnamon
Dash of ground cloves
1/2 teaspoon bourbon whiskey
1/2 teaspoon lime or lemon juce
4 fresh apricots*

Bakeware: 1 aluminum baking sheet to fit oven

Preheat convection oven at "Broil" according to oven directions. Stir together all ingredients except apricots. Cut apricots in half lengthwise (along seam) and twist to separate halves. Remove pits. Spread about 1 teaspoon of butter on cut edge of each half. Place apricot halves on baking sheet, leaving at least 1 inch of air space between halves. Slide sheet onto center rack of preheated oven and broil 5 to 10 minutes or until apricots are slightly soft.

Standard oven: Preheat 5 to 10 minutes at "Broil"; place halves on broiler rack and broil about 4 inches from heat 5 to 7 minutes.

*Fresh peaches or nectarines may be substituted for apricots.

convection braising and casserole cookery

BRAISING AND CASSEROLE COOKERY

Casseroles and braised dishes are first cousins. Unlike roasting and broiling, both of these categories of recipes utilize moisture. Casserole ingredients are mixed together or layered or assembled in a dish and then baked, while braised foods are usually browned first and then cooked in liquid until tender. Many recipes overlap and can be considered as belonging to both categories.

Both casseroles and braised foods can be cooked with pleasing results in a convection oven. Casseroles are among the easiest dishes to cook and do not need a great deal of explanation beyond recipe directions. Cooking casseroles in a convection oven is an easy transition from a conventional oven. Temperature is either maintained or lowered 25 degrees and time shortened by one fourth to one third.

While casseroles can be summed up simply, a discussion of braising is valuable because this cooking method involves more technique and can open up new doors to delicious and economical eating. Many braised dishes have European origins. Just think of all the braised dishes you can—stews, pot roasts, ragouts and goulashes—and you can think of a European country to go with each one. Braising was perfected in Europe, where few tender cuts of meat were available. Economics was originally the reason behind many of the braised dishes, such as coq au vin and pot-au-feu, that are now considered fancy restaurant fare in the United States.

ADVANTAGES OF BRAISING

Braising is the method of cooking food, usually meat and/or vegetables, in liquid. This moist-heat technique has many advantages:

● **Braising Is Economical Because It Utilizes Less-tender Cuts of Meat.** Because braising tenderizes tough cuts, less tender cuts of meat may be used. These have superb flavor and are less expensive than the tender cuts recommended for roasting and broiling. Almost any liquid can be used as a braising medium: water, stock, vegetable or fruit juice, wine or beer or any combination of two or more.

● **Braising Is Easy Because It Offers Ingredient Flexibility.** Once you have a feel for braising (which does not take long to acquire), you can add and subtract and multiply ingredients as you wish and come up with a new version of the same recipe each time you cook it. That's what makes braising so easy—and such fun! This flexibility also makes for economical cooking. You can go with the supermarket specials. If a recipe calls for beef stew meat but chuck roast is on sale, you can use the chuck roast. If a recipe calls for turnips but your grocer doesn't have them, substitute onions or add more carrots. If a recipe calls for three cups of beef stock and you have only two cups, make up the difference with tomato juice or water. To add character to braising liquids, add bones or a bouquet garni of parsley and bay leaves or vegetables of your choice.

● **Braised Foods Are Better the Second or Third Day.** Flavors blend and subtleties appear when braised dishes are cooked one to two days before serving. This makes braising ideal for "make ahead" cooking and means that braised foods are delicious as leftovers.

● **It's Very Difficult to Ruin a Braising Recipe.** Since liquid is present, it is difficult to burn braised foods, especially when the dish is cooked in an oven with constantly circulating hot air. Because several ingredients come together, it is almost impossible to end up with a tasteless dish. Because they make great leftovers, there is no waste with braised foods. If you wish, you can keep a large pot of beef bourguignon in the refrigerator for a week and draw off and reheat a portion of it each day until it is all gone.

BRAISING IN A CONVECTION OVEN

While many braising recipes call for range-top cooking, braised dishes can be cooked even better in an oven, because oven heat is more even than range-top heat and the chance of spot-scorching is thereby reduced. Braising in a convection oven is faster and more energy efficient than standard-oven braising. Some braising recipes can be assembled like casseroles, but most have two basic steps: browning and cooking in liquid.

In standard braising, meat can be browned in the braising pan over high heat on the range-top or under the broiler in the oven. There are also two options in convection braising: browning on the rack in a convection oven set at a high temperature; or browning in the braising pan on top of the range over high heat.

To brown in a convection oven, place the meat directly on the oven rack and slide into the preheated oven set at "Broil" or another high temperature. Cook until the meat is seared and browned, 20 to 30 minutes depending upon size of cut. Transfer meat to braising pot, add liquid and return to oven set at 325° to 350°F. Browning in the convection oven is practical only when it has two racks so that washing the rack between steps can be avoided. Brown meat on one rack and place braising pot on the second rack.

The alternative is browning the traditional way—on top of the range over high heat, which is often preferable. It is faster and it leaves some of those lovely brown bits in the bottom of the braising pan that add character and flavor to the finished dish. Meats can be browned in vegetable or olive oil, beef or pork drippings or butter or margarine mixed with a little vegetable oil to prevent burning. Use as little oil or fat as possible to keep dish from getting greasy. The most important things to remember about range-top browning are that you should not step away from it, since the high heat can scorch foods quickly, and that you should use tongs to turn and maneuver the meat so that it is browned on both the sides *and* the edges. This searing on top of the range allows range-top cooking to team up with convection cooking for the best possible result.

THE PROPER POT

Selecting the proper pot for braising is not difficult but it is crucial for speedy and successful cooking. There's a good chance you probably have the right pot in your kitchen already. The best braising pot is one that is flameproof and ovenproof—one that can go from top of the range to oven without fear of cracking, melting or warping. Aluminum or stainless steel all-metal pots with short handles and tight-fitting lids are best, and they are usually so durable that they can last for decades. Covered pots made of enameled cast iron or flameproof ceramic also work well. If you are shopping for a new pot, look for an all-aluminum one (for efficient and even heat transfer) with a non-stick lining. The most important factor to consider is size—the pot should fit in the oven leaving at least one inch of air space on all sides.

THE PARCHMENT PLOY

Any cook who has ever put a covered pot of stew on the range to simmer for a long period of time can attest to the fact that the lid of the pot and the sides of the pot above the food line collect spatters and usually end up being more difficult to clean than the pot below the food line. (This is especially true of tomato-based dishes.) In this instance, cleanup is the least of concerns. What has happened that is even more important is a certain loss of flavor that has become a residue on the sides and lid of the pot instead of staying in the liquid. There's a simple trick that helps concentrate flavors and keeps pots cleaner when braising, and all it involves is a piece of cooking parchment. Cut a circle (or oval) of parchment to fit inside the braising pot. After adding the liquid, place the parchment on top of the food in the pot, pressing it gently in place against the surface of the food. This will prevent the liquid condensing and evaporating in the space between the food and the lid. (Cooking parchment is available in gourmet shops and cookware departments.)

CONVECTION BRAISING GUIDELINES

● **Brown Meats Before Adding Liquid for Most Flavorful Results.**
● **Use a Non-Stick Pot to Minimize Greasiness.**
● **Use a Piece of Cooking Parchment to Top Foods Before Covering with Lid.** This helps concentrate flavors and makes cleanup easier.
● **To Test Meats and Vegetables for Doneness, Insert the Tip of a Small Knife.** A meat thermometer or instant-read thermometer generally is not needed for braising.
● **Reheat Braised Foods in Your Convection Oven.** Set the temperature control at 300° to 325°F for reheating. Transfer foods to a smaller pot, if necessary. All-metal, enameled cast iron or flameproof ceramic saucepans work well for reheating. Keep food covered or it will brown.

MEAT, CHICKEN AND FISH DISHES

YANKEE POT ROAST

An American classic.

Serves 4 to 6
One 2-1/2- to 3-pound beef chuck arm,
    shoulder or blade roast
2 tablespoons bacon drippings
1 small onion, chopped
1 teaspoon salt
1/4 teaspoon freshly ground pepper
4 cups beef stock
4 whole cloves
4 small onions, peeled
3 medium potatoes, peeled and halved
2 carrots, peeled and cut into 2-inch pieces
2 celery ribs, cut into 2-inch pieces
1 to 1-1/2 teaspoons salt
3 tablespoons all-purpose flour
5 tablespoons water
1 teaspoon beef seasoning base

Bakeware: One 5-quart flameproof Dutch oven

Preheat convection oven to 350°F. Brown roast on all sides in bacon drippings in Dutch oven over high heat. Remove roast to platter, add chopped onion to pot and stir over medium heat until golden, about 5 minutes. Return roast to pot, sprinkle with 1 teaspoon salt and pepper and pour 3 cups beef stock around roast. Bring to a boil, place circle of parchment paper cut to fit pot directly over roast, cover and place in preheated oven. Bake 1-1/2 hours, turning roast once after 45 minutes. Add beef stock as needed to keep roast almost covered. Insert 1 clove into each peeled onion. Add onions, potatoes, carrots, celery and remaining beef stock to pot around roast. Sprinkle vegetables with 1 to 1-1/2 teaspoons salt. Replace parchment and cover and bake 40 minutes more or until meat and vegetables are tender.

To make gravy, remove meat and vegetables to platter and keep warm in 150°F oven while making gravy. Skim excess grease from drippings in pot. Bring drippings to boil over high heat; boil about 5 minutes. In screwtop jar, shake flour and water until blended. Whisk into boiling drippings gradually. Stir in beef seasoning base. Boil gravy 2 minutes. Spoon small amount over meat and vegetables to glaze. Pass remaining gravy in gravyboat. Slice meat 1/4 inch thick to serve.

Standard oven: Preheat to 350°F; bake 1-1/2 to 1-3/4 hours, add vegetables and bake 1 hour.

BEEF BURGUNDY

An Americanized version of a classic French dish.

Serves 6 to 8
6 slices bacon, 1/8 inch thick
3 pounds beef stew meat, cut into 1-inch cubes
Olive oil (optional)
1 pound mushrooms, quartered
1 pound small white onions, peeled
2 teaspoons salt
1/4 teaspoon freshly ground pepper
3 cups red Burgundy wine
2 cups beef stock
1 tablespoon tomato paste
2 garlic cloves, crushed
1/2 teaspoon dried thyme leaves, crushed
2 bay leaves
4 tablespoons cornstarch

Bakeware: One 4- to 4-1/2-quart Dutch oven with lid

Preheat convection oven to 350°F. Cut bacon into 1/4-inch pieces and cook in Dutch oven over medium heat until crisp. Remove bacon pieces with a slotted spoon and set aside. Brown beef cubes in bacon drippings, adding olive oil if needed, and remove to a bowl. Brown mushrooms and onions in Dutch oven, pour off excess fat and return beef to pot. Add salt, pepper, bacon, wine, stock, tomato paste, garlic, thyme and bay leaves; stir and bring to a boil. Place circle of cooking parchment cut to fit inside Dutch oven directly on beef mixture. Cover and bake in center of preheated oven 1-1/4 to 1-3/4 hours or until beef is tender. After meat has cooked 1 hour, remove 1/2 cup cooking liquid to a small bowl and refrigerate to cool to room temperature. To thicken sauce, remove parchment and bring beef to a boil on stove burner. Stir cornstarch into cooled cooking liquid and gradually stir into the boiling beef. Boil 2 minutes. Serve with crusty French bread.

Standard oven: Preheat to 350°F; bake 2 to 2-1/4 hours.

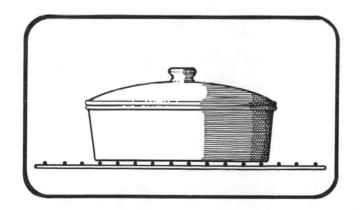

MOTHER'S PEPPER STEAK

A hearty entrée for cold winter evenings.

Serves 4
One 1-1/2-pound round-bone sirloin steak,
   3/4 inch thick
1/2 teaspoon salt
1/4 teaspoon onion powder
Freshly ground black pepper
1 can (14-1/2 ounces) whole tomatoes in
   tomato juice
1 medium onion, peeled, halved and sliced
2 celery ribs, cut into 2-inch pieces
3 carrots, peeled and cut into 2-inch pieces
1 cup coarsely chopped cabbage
1/2 cup green beans, cut into 2-inch pieces
1/2 pound mushrooms, sliced
2 green peppers, cut into 1-inch strips
1 teaspoon instant flour mixed with 1 tablespoon cold water (optional)

Bakeware: One 4-1/2- or 5-quart Dutch oven
with lid, to fit oven

Preheat convection oven to 350°F. Cut excess fat from sirloin steak and chop fat into pieces. Cut sirloin into 6 serving-sized pieces and sprinkle with salt, onion powder and pepper. Stir-fry fat in Dutch oven until bottom of pot is coated with grease; discard fat pieces. Brown meat on both sides in fat over high heat. If meat does not fit into pan in single layer, brown in 2 batches. Drain tomatoes, reserving juice. Chop tomatoes coarsely and add with tomato juice to meat in Dutch oven. Add onion, celery, carrots, cabbage and green beans. If liquid does not cover meat and vegetables, add additional tomato juice or beef stock. Bring to a simmer. Cut a circle of parchment paper to fit inside of Dutch oven. Place parchment directly over meat and vegetables and gently press into place. Cover and place in preheated oven. Bake 45 minutes. Add mushrooms and green peppers, replace parchment, cover and bake another 15 minutes. Serve as is or thicken gravy as follows: Remove meat and keep warm. Bring gravy in Dutch oven to a boil on range burner and stir in flour mixed with cold water. Return meat to pot and simmer 2 minutes. Serve with hot buttered noodles.

Standard oven: Preheat to 350°F; bake 50 minutes, add mushrooms and green peppers and bake 20 minutes.

VEAL ROAST BRAISED IN RED WINE

Red Bordeaux gives a hearty flavor to the veal and the sauce.

Serves 6 to 8
One 2-1/2- to 3-pound boned and rolled
   veal roast
1/2 teaspoons salt
1/2 teaspoon freshly ground pepper
2 tablespoons all-purpose flour
About 3 tablespoons olive oil
1 cup chopped yellow onions
1 cup chopped red onions
1/2 cup sliced celery (with some celery tops,
   if possible)
2 garlic cloves, crushed
1/4 teaspoon summer savory, crushed
1 sprig fresh rosemary, or 1/4 teaspoon dried
   rosemary leaves, crushed
1 sprig fresh thyme, or 1/4 teaspoon dried
   thyme leaves, crushed
2 bay leaves
1-1/2 cups red Bordeaux wine
1-1/2 cups beef broth
1 teaspoon beef seasoning base
1 tablespoon instant flour

Bakeware: One 3-1/2- to 4-quart Dutch oven
with lid

Preheat convection oven to 350°F. Pat veal dry with paper toweling, rub salt and pepper all over veal and dredge lightly with flour. Heat 2 tablespoons olive oil in Dutch oven until a haze forms and brown veal on all sides and ends in oil over medium high heat, turning with tongs. Remove veal to plate. Add onions, celery and garlic to Dutch oven and cook and stir over medium heat about 5 minutes or until onions begin to soften, adding more olive oil if needed. Stir summer savory, rosemary, thyme and bay leaves into vegetables and cook 1 to 2 minutes more. Place veal in pot on top of vegetables, pour wine and beef stock around roast. Bring to boil and cover roast with aluminum foil, molding foil around veal, down to liquid, up sides of the pot and over the edge of the pot. Cover with pot lid and cook in center of preheated oven 1 to 1-1/4 hours or until veal is tender.

Remove veal and aluminum foil to warm platter and keep warm while making gravy. Strain pan juices into medium saucepan, gently pressing juices from vegetables; reserve vegetables. Bring pan juices to a boil and boil vigorously 5 to 10 minutes, reducing liquid to about 1-1/2 cups. Stir in beef seasoning base, taste and season with salt and pepper. Whisk instant flour into boiling juices and continue to simmer gently 2 minutes. Stir in about 1 cup of the reserved vegetables. To serve, spoon a small amount of sauce over veal on serving platter, slice veal into 1/4-inch slices and pass sauce in gravyboat. Nice with Oven-roast Potatoes, page 88, or boiled new potatoes.

Standard oven: Preheat to 350°F; bake 1-1/4 to 1-3/4 hours.

STUFFED CABBAGE ROLLS IN DILL SAUCE

The sauce makes this everyday dish elegant enough for company fare.

Serves 6
1 small cabbage

FILLING
1 pound lean pork, cubed
2 ounces pork fat
1 slice bacon, cut into pieces
1/4 cup snipped parsley
2 tablespoons chopped shallots (about 2) or onion
1/4 cup half-and-half
1 egg yolk
1/4 cup soft bread crumbs
1-1/2 teaspoons Seasoned Salt, page 108
1 garlic clove, crushed
1/2 teaspoon dried thyme leaves, crushed
1/8 teaspoon freshly ground pepper

3 tablespoons butter or margarine
1/2 cup thinly sliced celery
1/2 cup thinly sliced carrots
1/2 cup chopped onion
1/4 cup dry white vermouth
1 cup beef stock
2 teaspoons cornstarch
3/4 cup Crème Fraîche, page 132, or whipping cream
3 tablespoons snipped fresh dill, or 1-1/2 tablespoons dried dill, crushed

Bakeware: 1 shallow flameproof casserole with lid, or au gratin dish and aluminum foil.

Preheat convection oven to 400°F. Cut core from cabbage but leave cabbage whole. Bring large pot of water to a boil, place cabbage in boiling water, return to boil, cover and boil about 6 minutes. Remove cabbage to bowl of cold water set in sink. When cool enough to handle, peel softened leaves from cabbage and place on paper toweling to drain. Repeat boiling and peeling until you have 16 whole leaves. Cut a triangular wedge from each leaf to remove thick stem portion. Set leaves aside.

To make filling, put pork, pork fat, bacon and parsley through meat grinder or process in food processor until finely chopped. Transfer to bowl. Add remaining filling ingredients and mix well. To form cabbage rolls, place dry leaf on work surface with triangular cutout closest to you. Spoon about 3 tablespoons filling onto center of leaf. Fold portion of leaf closest to you over filling, then fold in right and left sides and top edge. Set aside, seam side down. Repeat with all leaves and filling.

Melt butter in flameproof casserole. Cook celery, carrots and onion in butter over low heat until limp and glossy, about 15 minutes. Do not brown. Place cabbage rolls, seam sides down, on bed of vegetables. Pour vermouth and beef stock over cabbage rolls. Bring to a simmer over medium heat and cover with lid or aluminum foil molded to edge of pan. Place in preheated oven and reduce oven temperature to 350°F. Bake 25 minutes or until cabbage is tender and filling is firm. Remove from oven, place rolls on serving platter and keep warm in 150°F oven while making sauce. Set casserole with cooking liquid over high heat and boil vigorously 5 minutes. Stir cornstarch into crème fraîche, then stir crème fraîche into cooking juices. Add dill and simmer 2 minutes. Spoon sauce over cabbage rolls on platter. Serve with rice or buttered noodles.

Standard oven: Preheat to 400°F; reduce to 350°F and bake 30 minutes.

SIMPLY AMERICAN CASSOULET

A combination of corned beef, Polish sausage and beans makes for stick-to-the-ribs eating.

Serves 8 to 10
One 2-to 2-1/2-pound oven-roast corned beef brisket
1 to 1-1/2 pounds smoked Polish sausage
About 4-1/2 cups baked beans
1/3 cup packed brown sugar
1/4 cup catsup
2 tablespoons Dijon-style mustard
1/4 teaspoon dried thyme leaves, crushed
2 teaspoons Worcestershire sauce
2 cups seasoned bread crumbs

Bakeware: 1 oven rack with drip pan in place; 1 shallow 2-quart casserole, 12 × 7-1/2 × 2 inches.

Preheat convection oven to 325°F. Pat corned beef dry with paper toweling. Place on oven rack and slide rack ino center of preheated oven. Roast about 1 hour, then add Polish sausage to oven rack, leaving at least 1 inch of space between corned beef and sausage. Sausage can be cooked on separate rack, if desired. Continue to roast 20 to 30 minutes or until corned beef is tender and sausage is brown. Remove sausage before corned beef, if necessary. Remove drip pan from oven and turn temperature to 350°F. Allow meats to cool to handling temperature. Slice corned beef diagonally across the grain into 1/8- to 1/4-inch-thick slices and cut sausage into 1-inch-thick pieces. In medium saucepan, combine beans, brown sugar, catsup, mustard, thyme and Worcestershire sauce. Heat to boiling and pour half of the bean mixture into the casserole. Sprinkle half of the seasoned bread crumbs over the beans and arrange corned beef slices and Polish sausage pieces in overlapping pattern on beans. Pour remaining beans over meat to cover and sprinkle with remaining bread crumbs. Bake in preheated oven for 20 to 25 minutes or until beans are bubbly and crumbs are light brown. Nice served with crusty bread; see No-knead White Bread and Roll Yeast Dough, page 31.

Standard oven: Preheat to 325°F; roast corned beef about 1-1/4 hours before adding Polish sausage. Roast another 30 to 40 minutes before removing meat. Turn temperature to 350°F and bake casserole 30 to 35 minutes.

BRAISED PORK WITH PAPRIKA AND CARAWAY

Not only does this dish taste good—it also makes a beautiful presentation.

Serves 6 to 8

One 3-pound boneless pork loin roast, rolled and tied
2 tablespoons olive oil
1 cup chopped onion
1 cup sliced peeled carrots
1/2 cup sliced celery
1 teaspoon sweet paprika
1-1/4 cups chicken or beef stock
1 to 1-1/2 teaspoons salt
Freshly ground black pepper
1 teaspoon caraway seeds
2 tablespoons all-purpose flour
1 cup sour cream or Crème Fraîche, page 132
2 teaspoons capers, drained and chopped

Bakeware: One 4 to 4-1/2-quart flameproof ovenproof Dutch oven with lid

Preheat convection oven to 350°F. Pat pork dry with paper toweling. Heat oil in Dutch oven until haze forms, add pork and brown on all sides over medium high heat, turning pork with tongs, if possible. Remove pork to platter and pour off all but a thin film of fat. Add the onions and cook and stir over medium heat 3 to 4 minutes or until onions turn golden brown. Add carrots and celery and cook 3 to 4 minutes, stirring constantly. Remove pot from heat and stir paprika into vegetables. Add stock to pot, return to heat and bring to a boil, stirring to loosen any brown bits on the bottom or sides of pan. Place pork in pot fat side up and sprinkle with salt and pepper. Add caraway seeds to liquid around pork, sprinkling a few seeds on top of pork. Bring to a boil and cover pork with aluminum foil, molding foil around pork, down to liquid, up sides of pot and over edge of pot. Cover with pot lid, place in preheated oven and braise 1 to 1-1/4 hours or until pork is tender and instant-read thermometer registers at least 160°F.

Remove pork to heated platter and keep warm while making sauce. Strain pan juices into medium saucepan, pressing vegetables to extract their juices. Pour vegetables from strainer into a food mill fitted with a fine blade. Purée vegetables in food mill. (If a food mill is not available, press the vegetables through the strainer.) Set purée aside over very low heat to keep warm; discard caraway seeds and other remains in food mill. Skim fat from pan juices and bring to a boil over medium heat. Whisk flour into sour cream and whisk a small amount of hot pan juices into sour cream, then add sour cream to boiling juices all at once, whisking to blend completely. Simmer about 2 minutes. Stir in capers and any pork juices that have accumulated on platter. Taste and correct seasonings. To serve, slice pork 1/4 inch thick and top each serving with a few spoonfuls of sauce and a small dollop of puréed vegetables. Pass remaining sauce in gravyboat.

Standard oven: Preheat to 350°F; braise 1-1/2 to 1-3/4 hours.

SZEKELEY GULAS

An old Czechoslovakian favorite, this hearty casserole combines tart sauerkraut, rich sour cream and juicy pork.

Serves 4 to 6
1 can (8-1/4 ounces) whole tomatoes in juice
1/2 cup chopped onion
1 garlic clove, crushed
2 tablespoons vegetable oil
1 tablespoon all-purpose flour
1-1/2 teaspoons paprika
1 teaspoon salt
1/8 teaspoon cayenne pepper
1/2 teaspoon caraway seeds
1/2 teaspoon monosodium glutamate
   (optional)
2 pounds lean boneless pork, cut into
   1/2-inch cubes
1 tablespoon vegetable oil
1/4 cup water
1 can (16 ounces) sauerkraut, drained
1 cup sour cream mixed with 1 tablespoon
   all-purpose flour
Paprika

Bakeware: One 2-quart metal or glass casserole with lid.

Preheat convection oven to 350°F. Drain tomatoes, reserving liquid; chop tomatoes coarsely. Set aside. Cook onion and garlic in 2 tablespoons vegetable oil in 10-inch non-stick skillet over medium heat until onion is translucent. Remove onion mixture and reserve. Mix together flour, 1-1/2 teaspoons paprika, salt, pepper, caraway seeds and monosodium glutamate. Toss with pork cubes to coat. Add 1 tablespoon vegetable oil to hot skillet and brown meat in single layer over high heat. Remove from skillet and set aside. Add water and reserved tomato juice to skillet. Stir in sauerkraut, chopped tomatoes, reserved onion and sour cream-flour mixture (for a less sour flavor, rinse and drain sauerkraut before adding). Bring to a simmer. Layer one half of the pork, then one half of the sauerkraut in the 2-quart casserole. Layer remaining pork and sauerkraut, sprinkle with paprika and cover. Bake in preheated oven for 30 minutes. Remove cover and bake another 15 minutes. Serve with hot buttered noodles.

Standard oven: Preheat to 350°F; bake 45 minutes with cover, 15 minutes without.

SAUCY LEMON RIBS

Ribs are roasted, then braised in a spicy-sweet sauce that is excellent served over rice.

Serves 4
3 pounds pork back ribs
Salt
Freshly ground pepper
1 lemon, thinly sliced
1 large onion, thinly sliced

SAUCE
2 cups catsup
1/4 cup Worcestershire sauce
3/4 teaspoon chili powder
1-1/2 teaspoons salt
3 cups water
1/2 cup packed brown sugar

Bakeware: 1 or 2 aluminum jelly roll pans to fit oven; 1 or 2 roasting racks; 1 shallow 9 ×13-inch roasting pan

Preheat convection oven to 400°F. To remove membrane from back of rib slab, slide fork tine under membrane 1 rib away from small end of slab, pull up to loosen membrane, grasp with hand and pull off full length of slab. Cut slab into 3-rib pieces. Rub salt and pepper on both sides of ribs. Place on roasting rack on jelly roll pan, meaty side up. Place 1 lemon slice and 1 onion slice on each rib piece. Roast in pre-heated oven 30 to 40 minutes or until ribs are well browned and have rendered their fat. Transfer ribs to shallow roasting pan; discard fat.

While ribs are roasting make sauce: Combine sauce ingredients in medium saucepan and bring to a boil. Pour over ribs. If ribs are not covered by sauce, cover pan with aluminum foil, molding foil around edge of pan. Reduce oven temperature to 350°F and bake ribs until tender, about 40 to 45 minutes. If sauce does not cover ribs, baste 2 to 3 times. To serve, spoon small amount of sauce over ribs and pass remaining sauce. Delicious served with steamed rice.

Standard oven: Preheat to 425°F; roast ribs 30 to 40 minutes, reduce heat to 350°F; add sauce and braise about 1 hour.

HAM AND SPINACH ROLLS MORNAY

This make-ahead casserole can be served for brunch or, without English muffins, as a first course for dinner.

Serves 4 for brunch, 8 as a first course

HAM ROLLS
1 package (10 ounces) frozen chopped spinach
1/4 cup water
1/8 teaspoon garlic powder
1/4 teaspoon salt
4 tablespoons (1/2 stick) butter
1-1/2 tablespoons all-purpose flour
1 egg, lightly beaten
8 slices boiled ham, each 1/16 inch thick

MORNAY SAUCE
2 tablespoons butter
2 tablespoons all-purpose flour
1-1/4 cups milk
1/2 teaspoon salt
1/8 teaspoon freshly ground white pepper
Pinch of freshly grated nutmeg
1/4 cup shredded Gruyère or natural Swiss cheese

2 tablespoons grated Parmesan cheese
4 English muffins, split and toasted

Bakeware: One 6 × 10 × 2-inch glass or metal baking pan

To make ham rolls, cook spinach according to package directions using 1/4 cup water, garlic powder and salt. In separate saucepan, melt butter, add flour and cook and stir over medium heat until mixture bubbles for 2 minutes. Remove from heat. Add cooked spinach with liquid and stir to blend. Return to heat, bring to a boil and quickly stir in beaten egg. Set aside and cool enough to handle. To fill rolls, spoon 3 tablespoons spinach filling across each ham slice, roll up and place seam side down in well-buttered baking pan in a single row. Preheat convection oven to 350°F.

To make Mornay sauce, melt butter in small saucepan, add flour and cook and stir over medium heat until mixture bubbles 2 minutes. Remove from heat. Whisk in milk until blended. Return to heat and bring to a boil over medium heat, stirring constantly. Add salt, pepper and nutmeg and simmer 2 minutes. Stir in Gruyère, taste and correct seasonings. Pour over ham rolls in baking pan. Sprinkle on Parmesan. (Make ahead note: Casserole may be refrigerated overnight at this point. If using glass baking pan, bring to room temperature before baking.) Bake in preheated oven 10 to 15 minutes or until sauce bubbles and cheese just begins to brown. Serve 2 rolls over each split, toasted English muffin. A fresh fruit cup is a lovely accompaniment for brunch. To serve as a first course, omit English muffins and serve 1 roll per person.

Standard oven: Preheat to 350°F; bake 20 minutes.

CHICKEN IN MOSELLE WITH MUSHROOMS ☆

Chicken is braised in stock and wine, then sauced with cream. Serve the same wine with dinner that is used in the sauce.

Serves 4

1 broiler-fryer, cut up
4 tablespoons (1/2 stick) unsalted butter or margarine
1 tablespoon olive oil
1/2 cup finely chopped shallots (about 5) or onion
1 tablespoon all-purpose flour
1 cup Moselle wine
1 cup chicken stock
1/2 teaspoon salt
1/8 teaspoon freshly ground pepper
1 teaspoon dried rosemary leaves
1 bay leaf

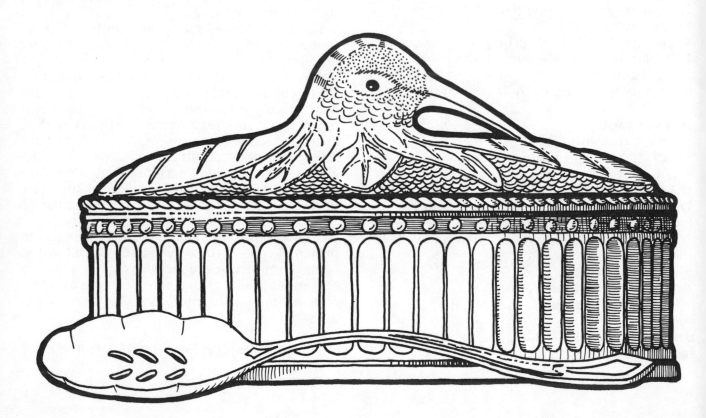

MUSHROOM GARNISH

1/2 pound mushrooms, quartered
1 tablespoon lemon juice
3 tablespoons unsalted butter or margarine
1 teaspoon sugar
Pinch of salt

1 cup whipping cream or Crème Fraîche,
  page 132
1 teaspoon lemon juice
1 tablespoon all-purpose flour blended with
  2 tablespoons water (optional)
2 tablespoons snipped parsley

Bakeware: One 4-1/2- or 5-quart Dutch oven with lid, to fit oven

Preheat convection oven to 350°F. Cut a circle of cooking parchment to fit inside Dutch oven; set aside. Cook chicken in butter and olive oil in Dutch oven over medium heat until brown on all sides. Remove chicken pieces and set aside. Cook shallots in pan drippings, stirring constantly until shallots are tender, about 3 minutes. Stir in flour, scraping up any brown bits on the bottom of pan. Stir in wine, chicken stock, salt, pepper, rosemary and bay leaf. Heat to boiling. Add chicken pieces to pot, placing dark meat pieces in bottom of pot. Top chicken with circle of cooking parchment, pressing gently against chicken. Cover and place in preheated oven. Bake about 25 minutes or until chicken is fork-tender.

While chicken is in oven, make mushroom garnish: Sprinkle 1 tablespoon lemon juice over mushrooms. Cook mushrooms in 2 tablespoons butter in non-stick skillet over medium-high heat, tossing constantly until mushrooms are golden and glossy, about 5 minutes. Sprinkle sugar and pinch of salt over mushrooms and continue to toss over heat until mushrooms are glazed. Set aside.

Transfer chicken to serving platter; cover and keep warm in 150°F oven while making sauce. Strain pan juices into saucepan. Skim off excess fat. Bring to rolling boil over high heat and boil until liquid is reduced to about 1-1/2 cups. Stir in whipping cream and 1 teaspoon lemon juice. Taste and correct seasonings. For thicker sauce, whisk in flour blended with water. Boil until thickened, about 2 minutes. Stir in mushrooms. Pour sauce over chicken. Sprinkle on parsley. Serve with rice or boiled potatoes and remaining Moselle wine.

Standard oven: Preheat to 350°F; bake 30 to 35 minutes.

CHINESE BRAISED WHITEFISH

Adapted from the repertoire of Chu Yen and Pansy Luke, Chinese cooks extraordinaire!

Serves 4
One 1-1/2- to 2-pound whitefish or red snapper, cleaned and dressed
1-1/2 teaspoons salt
1/8 teaspoons monosodium glutamate (optional)
1/8 teaspoon freshly ground black pepper
2 tablespoons fermented black beans*
2 tablespoons chopped ginger root*
2 garlic cloves, chopped
2 tablespoons peanut oil
4 tablespoons soy sauce
4 tablespoons Chinese sweet cooking wine* or sherry
1 green onion, chopped

Bakeware: One 9 × 13 × 2-inch metal or glass baking pan

Preheat convection oven to 325°F. With sharp knife, score fish diagonally almost to bone on both sides. Mix together salt, monosodium glutamate and pepper; sprinkle in fish cavity and slits and over fish. Soak black beans in cool water about 5 minutes. Remove beans from water with fingers to drain; chop. Chop together beans, ginger and garlic until very fine. Stuff cavity and slits of fish with mixture. Place fish in baking pan. Pour peanut oil, then soy sauce over fish. Pour cooking wine around fish and stir gently to blend. Sprinkle green onion in liquid around fish. Cover pan with aluminum foil, molding foil to edge of pan. Bake in preheated oven 25 to 30 minutes or until fish flakes easily with fork. Serve with steamed rice.

Standard oven: Preheat to 350°F; bake about 30 minutes.

*Available at Oriental food markets or in Chinese sections of some supermarkets.

JAMBALAYA

Braised rice enhanced with shrimp, ham and bacon from the heart of the South.

Serves 4 to 6
1/4 pound sliced bacon, cut into 1-inch pieces
1/2 cup chopped onion
1 to 2 garlic cloves, crushed
1 large sweet green pepper, seeded and cut into 1/2-inch strips
2 tablespoons minced parsley
1/2 pound cooked smoked ham, cut into 1/2 × 1/2 × 1-1/2-inch strips
1 cup raw rice
1 can (1 pound, 3 ounces) whole-pack tomatoes, drained and coarsely chopped (juice reserved)
1/2 teaspoon dried thyme leaves, crushed
1 teaspoon salt
Freshly ground black pepper
1-1/2 to 2 cups chicken stock
1 pound raw medium shrimp, shelled and deveined

Bakeware: One 3- to 4-quart flameproof oven-proof Dutch oven with lid

Preheat convection oven to 350°F. Cook bacon in Dutch oven over medium heat until fat is rendered and bacon is brown but not crisp. Remove bacon and reserve. Add onions to pot and cook and stir until onions are translucent, about 5 minutes. Stir in the garlic, green pepper, half the parsley and the ham; cook and stir until peppers wilt, about 3 minutes. Add rice and stir to coat with fat; cook and stir until rice turns milky white, 2 to 3 minutes. Add the tomatoes and their juice, thyme, salt, pepper and chicken stock. Bring to a boil, place cooking parchment circle directly on top of rice, cover and bake in center of preheated oven 15 to 18 minutes. Add shrimp to pot, pushing them down into rice mixture; cover and return to oven for another 5 to 7 minutes. To serve, heap onto large heated platter and sprinkle with remaining parsley.

Standard oven: Preheat to 350°F; bake 20 minututes before adding shrimp and 7 to 8 minutes after.

VEGETABLE, RICE AND PASTA DISHES

CREAMY CARROT CASSEROLE ☆

A special-occasion vegetable dish with a vibrant, fresh color and subtle carrot flavor.

Serves 6 to 8
1-1/2 to 2 pounds carrots, peeled and cut into chunks
About 1 tablespoon salt
1/2 cup Crème Fraîche, page 132
4 tablespoons (1/2 stick) butter
4 tablespoons bourbon whiskey
Pinch of freshly grated nutmeg

Bakeware: One 1-quart ceramic or metal casserole

Preheat convection oven to 325°F. Cook carrots uncovered in large pot of boiling salted water until tender, about 15 minutes. Drain and purée in food processor, blender or food mill. Add all remaining ingredients. Taste and correct seasoning. Turn carrot mixture into greased casserole. Bake in preheated oven about 15 minutes or until purée firms up slightly.

Standard oven: Preheat to 350°F; bake about 20 minutes.

SAUERKRAUT CASSEROLE

Mushrooms and sauerkraut make a surprisingly delightful combination in this mellow-flavored casserole.

Serves 6 to 8
2 cans (14 ounces each) sauerkraut
1/4 pound (1 stick) butter or margarine
1 large onion, chopped (about 1 cup)
1-1/2 cups chopped mushrooms
Salt
Freshly ground black pepper

Bakeware: One 1-1/2-quart glass or ceramic casserole

Preheat convection oven to 325°F. Bring sauerkraut to a boil in medium saucepan over medium heat, then reduce heat and simmer about 10 minutes. While sauerkraut is cooking, melt butter in large skillet and cook onions in butter over medium heat about 5 minutes; add mushrooms and continue to cook another 3 to 4 minutes or until onions and mushrooms are tender. Drain sauerkraut well and stir into skillet mixture. Pour into casserole and bake in center of preheated oven about 15 minutes or until slightly bubbly. To prepare ahead, use freezer-to-oven casserole, assemble ingredients and refrigerate. Increase baking time to 30 minutes.

Standard oven: Preheat to 350°F; bake 15 to 20 minutes or 30 to 40 minutes after refrigeration.

CHEESY SCALLOPED POTATOES ☆

This rich and filling potato dish fits into almost any buffet party plan.

Serves 8 to 10
2 to 2-1/2 pounds red potatoes, peeled and sliced 1/8 inch thick
4 to 5 green onions, sliced 1/4 inch thick (about 1 cup)
2 cups shredded Gruyère or natural Swiss cheese
3 tablespoons snipped parsley
2 eggs
1-1/2 cups half-and-half
1 teaspoon salt
1/4 teaspoon freshly ground white pepper
1/4 cup grated Parmesan cheese
2 tablespoons butter or margarine, cut into small pieces

Bakeware: One 12 × 7 × 2-inch glass or metal baking pan

Preheat convection oven to 325°F. Layer potato slices, green onions, 1-1/2 cups of the Gruyère cheese and snipped parsley in greased baking pan. Beat together eggs, half-and-half, salt and pepper. Pour over potato layers. Mix together remaining Gruyère and Parmesan cheese and sprinkle over potato mixture. Dot with butter. Cover with aluminum foil molded to edge of pan. Bake in preheated oven 20 minutes; remove foil and bake another 20 to 25 minutes or until potatoes are tender.

Standard oven: Preheat to 350°F; bake 30 minutes covered and 30 minutes uncovered.

AROMATIC POTATOES ANNA ☆

An interesting twist on a classic French dish.

Serves 6 to 8
6 tablespoons butter or margarine, melted
1-1/2 to 2 pounds Idaho potatoes
Salt
Freshly ground white pepper
2 tablespoons minced shallots or onion

Bakeware: One 8-inch round (2 inches deep) straight-sided aluminum cake pan or tart pan

Preheat convection oven to 400°F. Cut circle of cooking parchment to fit bottom of cake pan. Brush bottom and sides of pan with melted butter. Place parchment circle in bottom of pan and brush parchment with melted butter. Set aside and reserve remaining melted butter. Peel potatoes and slice 1/16 inch thick. Arrange overlapping slices in attractive pattern in bottom of cake pan. Drizzle generously with melted butter, sprinkle with salt, pepper and about 1 teaspoon minced shallots. Continue to layer potatoes, butter, seasonings and shallots, ending with a potato layer. (You do not need to arrange potatoes in attractive design after first layer.) Cover with aluminum foil pressed directly against potatoes. Bake in center of preheated oven for 30 minutes. Remove foil and bake another 15 minutes. Remove from oven and unmold as follows: Invert serving platter on cake pan, turn over, lift off cake pan and gently peel off parchment. Cut into wedges to serve.

Standard oven: Preheat to 425°F; bake 40 minutes with foil, 15 minutes without.

RISOTTO (Rice Braised in Chicken Stock)

Once you cook rice this way, you'll make it often.

Serves 6
1 tablespoon olive oil
2 tablespoons butter or margarine
1/2 cup finely chopped onion
1 cup long-grain rice
2 cups chicken stock
1 teaspoon salt
Freshly ground white pepper to taste
1 bay leaf, 2 sprigs parsley and 1/4 teaspoon dried thyme leaves tied in cheesecloth (bouquet garni)

Bakeware: One 1-1/2- to 2-quart ovenproof saucepan

Preheat convection oven to 350°F. Heat olive oil and butter in saucepan until sizzling hot. Add onion and cook and stir over medium heat until onion is soft but not brown, about 5 minutes. Add rice and stir over medium heat until each grain turns opaque, about 3 minutes. (This step burns off the starchy outer coating and makes the rice fluffy.) Add chicken stock, salt, pepper and bouquet garni. Stir once, bring to a simmer, cover and place in center of preheated oven. Bake 15 to 20 minutes or until stock is absorbed and rice is tender. (Do not peek during first 15 minutes of baking.) Remove bouquet garni before serving. For even fluffier rice, stir, replace cover and let stand 10 minutes before serving.

Standard oven: Preheat to 350°F; bake 15 to 20 minutes.

STUFFED MANICOTTI WITH MEAT SAUCE

An Italian favorite that can be served as a first course or entrée.

Serves 8 as a first course, 4 as an entrée

SAUCE
1 pound ground beef
2 garlic cloves, crushed
1/2 cup chopped onion
2 cans (6 ounces each) tomato paste
2 cups water
2 tablespoons snipped parsley
1 tablespoon dried basil, crushed
1-1/2 teaspoons salt
1/8 teaspoon freshly ground pepper
Pinch of sugar

FILLING
1-1/2 pounds ricotta cheese
2/3 cup grated Parmesan cheese
2 eggs
1/4 cup snipped parsley
1/2 teaspoon salt
Pinch of freshly ground pepper
Pinch of freshly grated nutmeg

8 manicotti shells
1/3 cup grated Parmesan cheese

Bakeware: One 12 × 7 × 2-inch glass or metal baking pan

Preheat convection oven to 325°F. To make sauce, brown meat over high heat in large skillet. Drain off excess fat. Add remaining sauce ingredients to skillet, bring to a boil, reduce heat, cover and simmer about 30 minutes, stirring occasionally. To make filling, purée ricotta cheese in food processor or blender or put through food mill. Combine with remaining filling ingredients. Correct seasonings in sauce and filling. Cook manicotti shells in boiling water according to package directions until just tender. Rinse in cold water and drain. With pastry bag fitted with 1/2-inch tip or with small spoon, fill shells with ricotta filling. Pour half the sauce into baking pan and arrange filled manicotti in a row in pan. Top with remaining sauce. Sprinkle with 1/3 cup Parmesan. Bake in preheated oven 25 to 30 minutes or until sauce is bubbly and cheese has melted.

Standard oven: Preheat to 350°F; bake 30 to 35 minutes.

Note: Dish may be assembled and refrigerated several hours before baking. Increase baking time to 40 to 45 minutes in convection oven, 45 to 50 minutes in standard oven.

basic recipes

DUCK STOCK

Makes about 1 cup
Neck and giblets from 1 duck
3 cups water
1 celery top
1 carrot, peeled and diced
2 shallots or 1/2 small onion, peeled and
    quartered
6 peppercorns
1 teaspoon dried thyme leaves
1/2 teaspoon dried rosemary leaves
1 bay leaf
Salt
Freshly ground pepper

Place all ingredients in 3-quart saucepan. Bring to a boil, skim off scum, reduce heat and simmer 45 to 50 minutes, adding water as needed to keep ingredients barely covered. Strain stock into small saucepan, heat to boiling and reduce to about 1 cup. Taste and season with salt and pepper.

To be used in:
Roast Duckling with Cherry Brandy Sauce
Roast Duck with Gravy

CRÈME FRAÎCHE (French Double Cream)

A rich cream for sauces, fillings and toppings that lends an authentic flavor to French recipes.

Makes about 1-1/3 cups
1 cup whipping cream
2-1/2 tablespoons buttermilk, or 1/3 cup
    cultured sour cream

In screw-top jar or plastic container, stir together ingredients until well blended. Let stand at room temperature, loosely covered, 8 to 24 hours or until very thick (thickening time will depend on room temperature). Stir, cover and refrigerate. Should keep in refrigerator 10 days.

Note: Crème fraîche made with buttermilk is more tart than that made with sour cream. Both have a lovely, full flavor. Try each and take your pick.

To be used in:
Stuffed Cabbage Rolls in Dill Sauce
Molded Ham and Leek Quiche
Creamy Carrot Casserole
Chicken in Moselle with Mushrooms
Braised Pork with Paprika and Caraway
Cranberried Baked Apples
Roast Chicken with Tarragon Cream Sauce
Cheddar Cheese Tartlets
Creamy Cheesecake
This n' That Pastries

CRÈME CHANTILLY

Use in place of plain whipped cream as a dessert topping.

Makes about 1 cup
1/2 cup whipping cream
1/4 teaspoon vanilla extract

Beat whipping cream with chilled beaters until saucy consistency is reached. Blend in vanilla.

To be used on:
Free-Form Apple Tart
Georgia Derby Pie
The Ultimate Chocolate Cake

HORSERADISH SAUCE

Makes about 1-1/4 cups
1 cup sour cream, or 1/2 cup sour cream and
    1/2 cup whipping cream, whipped
1/3 cup prepared horseradish, drained
2 teaspoons fresh minced dill weed, or
    1 teaspoon dried dill weed
1/2 teaspoon salt
1/4 teaspoon freshly ground black pepper

Combine all ingredients and refrigerate at least 4 hours before serving.

To be served with:
Standing Rib Roast

PIZZA SAUCE

Make this tasty sauce ahead and freeze for future use.

Makes 3 cups (enough for 6 pizzas)
2 cans (16 ounces each) Italian plum whole-
    pack tomatoes
3 tablespoons olive oil
1 cup finely chopped onion
1 tablespoon minced garlic (3 to 4 cloves)
1 can (6 ounces) tomato paste
1 tablespoon dried oregano, crushed
2 teaspoons dried basil, crushed
1 large bay leaf
2 teaspoons sugar
1 tablespoon salt
1/4 teaspoon freshly ground black pepper

Drain tomatoes, reserving juice; chop tomatoes. Heat olive oil in enamel or stainless steel sauce-pan, add onion and cook and stir over medium heat about 7 minutes or until onions are tender. Add garlic and cook 2 minutes more, stirring constantly. Stir in tomatoes with their juice, and remaining ingredients. Bring to a boil, reduce heat to low and simmer uncovered for about 1 hour, stirring occasionally. Taste, correct seasonings and remove bay leaf. Freeze in 1/2-cup packets. Thaw and use as needed.

To be used in:
Neopolitan Pizza
Cheddar Cheese Tartlets
English Muffin Pizzas

PIZZA DOUGH

This dough, which may be made by hand or with a heavy-duty electric mixer, is so good that pizza crusts are never left on the plate. It makes interesting breadsticks, too.

Makes three 9 × 12-inch pizzas
2 packages active dry yeast
Pinch sugar
1/4 cup lukewarm water (110° to 115°F)
3-1/2 cups unbleached all-purpose flour
1-1/2 teaspoons salt
1 cup lukewarm water (110° to 115°F)
1/4 cup olive oil
Additional flour
1 tablespoon olive oil

Stir yeast and sugar into 1/4 cup lukewarm water. Set aside in warm place until yeast bubbles and doubles in volume, about 10 minutes. Stir together flour and salt in large mixing bowl. Make well in center of flour and pour in yeast, 1 cup lukewarm water and 1/4 cup olive oil. Mix until a rough ball forms. Place on floured pastry board and knead by hand for about 10 minutes, or knead with electric mixer fitted with dough hook, adding flour gradually if dough is sticky. After kneading, dough should be shiny and elastic. Rub inside of clean mixing bowl with 1 tablespoon olive oil. Place dough in bowl, turn oiled side up, cover with towel and let rise in warm place for 1 to 1-1/2 hours or until dough has doubled. Punch down and divide into 3 equal pieces. Assemble pizza immediately or wrap and freeze. Dough may rise slightly in freezer or while thawing; punch down before shaping.

To be used in:
Neopolitan Pizza
Crunchy Breadsticks
Pepperoni Cheese Appetizers

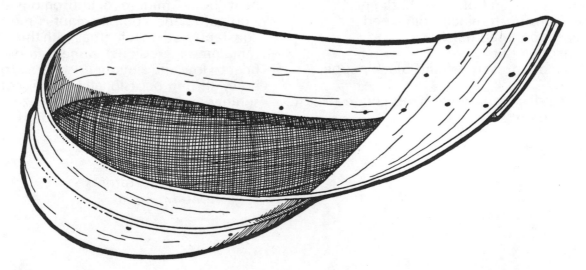

BASIC PIE DOUGH

Specially formulated for convection baking, this recipe can be made by hand or in a food processor and is easy to handle even for beginners.

Makes one 9-inch single pie crust or tart shell
1-1/2 cups unbleached all-purpose flour
1 teaspoon salt
2 teaspoons sugar (optional: for sweet dough only)
6 tablespoons unsalted butter or margarine, chilled
1 package (3 ounces) cream cheese, chilled
1 large egg, slightly beaten

To assemble by hand, combine flour, salt and sugar (optional) in mixing bowl. Cut butter and cream cheese into 1/4-inch dice and add to dry ingredients in bowl. With fingers or pastry blender, work ingredients together until mixture resembles coarse meal. Add the egg and work first with a fork and then by hand until dough comes together in a ball. Do not be afraid to squeeze or blend dough: It should have a smooth consistency. Flatten into patty shape, wrap in plastic and refrigerate one half hour to 1 hour before using.

To assemble in food processor, place flour, salt and sugar (optional) in bowl fitted with steel blade. Process 2 seconds to blend. Cut butter and cream cheese into chunks and add to processor bowl. Process with on-and-off motion until butter pieces are the size of very small peas. With processor running, pour egg into bowl through feed tube and continue to process until dough forms a ball. If ball appears to have pieces of butter or cream cheese in it, process an additional 5 to 10 seconds to get smooth consistency. If dough is sticky, add an additional 1 tablespoon flour and process 3 to 4 seconds. Flatten into patty shape, wrap in plastic and refrigerate one half hour to 1 hour before using.

To be used in:
Lattice-Top Apple Pie

UNBAKED PIE CRUST

1 recipe Basic Pie Dough, preceding

Roll out Basic Pie Dough on lightly floured surface to a thickness of 1/8 inch. Roll onto rolling pin and unroll over one 9-inch metal pie pan. Ease dough into pie pan and trim away excess dough with kitchen shears, leaving an extra 1/2 inch to shape edge. Gather up scraps, wrap and refrigerate. (Use scraps to make This 'n That Pastries, page 38.) Turn dough under 1/2 inch all around edge and pinch edge with a pastry crimper or press edge with the tines of a fork. Refrigerate until ready to use or wrap and freeze up to 1 week. It is not necessary to thaw frozen crust before filling.

To be used in:
Georgia Derby Pie
Streusel Peach Pie
This 'n That Pastries

FRENCH PASTRY DOUGH (Pâte Brisée)

A big-batch dough for tartlets, quiches and pies that is easy to handle and freezes well.

2 teaspoons salt
3-1/2 cups unbleached all-purpose flour
1/2 pound (2 sticks) unsalted butter, very cold
1/2 cup hydrogenated vegetable shortening
1 large egg
1/2 cup ice water
Flour

Add salt to flour and mix. Cut butter and shortening into chunks, add to flour and cut into flour with pastry blender or blending fork until mixture looks like coarse meal. Stir together egg and 1/2 cup ice water. Make well in center of flour, add egg mixture, stir with fork, then work with fingers to form ball. If dough is sticky, sprinkle on additional flour a tablespoon at a time until dough is no longer sticky. Divide dough in half. Flatten each half into a 1- to 2-inch thick circle, wrap and refrigerate 20 to 30 minutes before using. (Dough can be frozen at this point. To use frozen dough, remove to refrigerator section 1 day before using, or thaw frozen dough in convection oven, see page 140.) If dough becomes too soft to work at any time, return it to refrigerator for 10 minutes before proceeding.

Note: To make French Pastry Dough in a food processor, make half a recipe at a time in a small-bowl food processor or the full recipe all at once in large-bowl model.

To be used in:
Cheddar Cheese Tartlets
Extra-cheesy Quiche
This 'n That Pastries
Fruit Tart with Pastry Cream

BAKED PIE CRUST

Makes one 9-inch pie crust
1 recipe Basic Pie Dough, page 135
About 4 cups dried beans or rice

Bakeware: One 9-inch metal pie pan

Follow directions for Unbaked Pie Crust, page 135, up to point of refrigeration. Prick bottom and sides of pie crust with fork, then refrigerate 30 minutes before baking. Preheat convection oven to 400°F. Completely line the inside of pie crust with a circle of waxed paper and fill crust with dry beans, gently pushing beans against side of crust all around. Return to refrigerator for 5 minutes. Bake in center of preheated oven about 12 minutes or until edge looks set and begins to turn brown. Remove crust from oven, spoon out beans, remove waxed paper and prick bottom of crust again. Return to oven and continue to bake for an additional 10 to 15 minutes or until crust is brown and crisp. If edge is browning but bottom of crust appears pale and undercooked, slide pie crust out of pie pan directly onto oven rack and bake 5 to 10 minutes more, watching carefully to prevent over-browning of edge. Cool before filling.

To be used in:
Fresh Strawberry Pie

TOASTED GARLIC BREAD

A crunchy accompaniment for Italian entrées, such as Stuffed Manicotti with Meat Sauce.

Serves 4 to 6
8 to 12 slices Italian bread, 1 inch thick
2 to 3 garlic cloves, crushed
4 tablespoons olive oil
8 to 12 slices Italian bread, 1 inch thick

Bakeware: 1 or 2 racks with drip pan in place

Preheat convection oven to 325°F. Stir garlic into olive oil and brush oil on both sides of each slice of bread. Place slices on 1 or 2 oven racks, leaving at least 1 inch of space around each slice. Slide rack(s) into preheated oven and bake 15 to 20 minutes or until slices are light brown.

Standard oven: Preheat to 325°F; bake slices on baking sheet in center of oven for 15 minutes, turn slices over and bake another 15 minutes.

HERBES DE PROVENCE

In the South of France, you can find this fragrant blend of herbs everywhere. But alas, it is available only from certain shops here in the United States. This is not really a problem since just about every American spice rack contains the dried ingredients that make up Herbes de Provence. Simca, who lives in the heart of Provence, gave me a simple formula for remembering evermore the ingredients and proportions needed to mix an authentic blend: M-O-T-T-S—marjoram, oregano, thyme and summer savory! The double T stands for two parts thyme to one part of everything else. You can add a small amount of crushed bay leaf, which isn't in the code but is delicious in the blend.

Makes about 1/4 cup
2 teaspoons fresh or dried marjoram leaves
2 teaspoons fresh or dried oregano leaves
4 teaspoons fresh or dried thyme leaves
2 teaspoons fresh or dried summer savory leaves
1 teaspoon crushed dried bay leaf (optional)

Mix all herbs together and crush briefly in mortar with pestle. Store in airtight container in cool dark place.

To be used in:
Molded Ham and Leek Quiche
Baked Stuffed Fish
Herbed Broiled Pork Chops
Glazed Roasted Turkey

FRESH ROASTED NUTS

Buying raw nuts and roasting them freshly as they are needed makes a most delicious difference. They may be used for baking, in stir-fried dishes or salted and used for snacking.

Preheat convection oven to 325°F. Sprinkle raw nuts on ungreased baking sheet and roast in preheated oven according to this timetable until golden brown:

Type of Nut	Roasting Time
Spanish peanuts, with or without skins	20-25 minutes
Virginia peanuts	12-15 minutes
Whole cashews	8-12 minutes
Cashew pieces	6-10 minutes
Whole blanched almonds	14-16 minutes
Slivered blanched almonds	10-14 minutes
Chopped unblanched almonds	6-10 minutes

Cool completely before using.

Standard oven: Preheat to 325°F; increase roasting times above by 5 minutes. Watch carefully for scorching.

SEASONED SALT

Makes 6 to 7 tablespoons
2 tablespoons salt
1 tablespoon paprika
1 tablespoon ground turmeric
1 tablespoon onion powder
1-1/2 teaspoons garlic powder
1-1/2 teaspoons celery seeds, crushed
3/4 teaspoon freshly ground white pepper
3/4 teaspoon sugar
3/4 teaspoon ground thyme

Stir together all ingredients. For a finer texture and smoother blend, crush ingredients together in mortar with pestle. Store in airtight container.

GLAZED GRAPES

A beautiful edible garnish for poultry and ham.

1 bunch green grapes
2 egg whites, slightly beaten
Superfine sugar

With kitchen scissors, snip grapes into small clusters. Dip each cluster in beaten egg white, drain off excess white and roll in sugar to coat grapes. Place in single layer on waxed paper until coating is set, about 1 hour. Use immediately.

convection non-cooking

Setting the temperature control at "Off" would render most ovens useless. But that's not the case with convection ovens. With the air flow in operation and the temperature off, a convection oven creates a chamber of circulating air that is very helpful in accomplishing both food-related and non-food-related tasks.

While the following functions may not on their own warrant purchase of a convection oven, they are useful bonuses: thawing/defrosting, softening, crafting (using a convection oven as a craft tool), and dehydrating.

THAWING/DEFROSTING

While convection thawing is not as fast as microwave thawing, it is considerably faster than room-temperature or refrigerator thawing. In fact, convection thawing takes one third to one half the time of thawing a frozen product at room temperature. It saves even more time over thawing foods in the refrigerator—convection thawing takes from one eighth to one tenth the time of refrigerator thawing. Thickness determines the time needed to defrost frozen foods: The thicker the item, the longer the defrosting time. Follow this outline for fast, successful thawing:

CONVECTION THAWING PROCEDURE

● Use a convection oven for thawing *only if* the temperature control can be turned to "Off" or "0." Foods should not be thawed in any degree of heat, but rather in circulating cool air for the greatest safety and maximum quality.

● To save energy and speed defrosting time, wrap foods individually before freezing so they can easily be spread in a single layer during thawing.

● Place *wrapped* frozen foods on a rack in the center of the oven, leaving at least one inch of air space between items. If food is double wrapped, remove outer wrap or box. *Do not* stack foods; arrange in a single layer. Use more than one oven rack if necessary.

● When thawing steaks and chops before cooking, thaw only until they loose their rigidity. This will yield juicier steaks and chops, as a completely defrosted piece of meat tends to lose natural juices during cooking.

● Consult the following thawing timetable for approximate thawing times of popular foods.

CONVECTION THAWING TIMETABLE

FROZEN FOOD	THAWING TIME
Steaks	45 minutes per 1/2 inch
Chops	45 minutes per 1/2 inch
Ground meat patties	30 to 45 minutes per 1/2 inch
Ground meat, 1-pound block	1-1/2 to 2 hours
Slab of ribs, 1 inch thick	1-1/2 to 2 hours
Chicken pieces	45 to 60 minutes per 1/2 pound
Whole chicken, 3 pounds	3 to 4 hours
Bacon, 1-pound package	1-1/4 to 1-1/2 hours
Vegetables, 10-ounce package	45 to 60 minutes
Fruit, 10-ounce package	45 to 60 minutes
Orange juice and other fruit juice concentrates	
6-ounce can	20 to 30 minutes
12-ounce can	40 to 60 minutes
Pastry dough, 1-inch-thick block	20 to 30 minutes

SOFTENING

Only a few foodstuffs need softening before being incorporated into recipes or served. But those that do are crucial to successful results in many recipes. Is there a cook alive who has not wanted to bake a batch of cookies that begin with the "cream soft butter" step only to realize the butter is hard as a rock and will take long to soften? Probably not. A convection oven can turn exasperation into a sigh of relief.

In addition to the softening of butter and cream cheese, a convection oven is very useful in bringing refrigerated cheeses to a more pleasant temperature and texture for serving. Many cheeses straight from the refrigerator are too cold to yield their full delicious flavors and too firm to cut easily. Popping them into the circulating air of a convection oven for a short time does the trick faster than letting cheese sit at room temperature.

CONVECTION SOFTENING PROCEDURE

- Place food on oven rack.
- Slide rack into center of oven.
- Turn temperature control to "Off" or "0" and turn on oven to start air flow.
- Consult the following times for softening foods.

CONVECTION SOFTENING TIMETABLE

Stick of refrigerated butter	15 to 25 minutes
Stick of frozen butter	About 1 hour
Refrigerated cream cheese, 3-ounce package	20 to 25 minutes
Refrigerated cream cheese, 8-ounce package	30 to 40 minutes
Hard cheese (Swiss, Edam, etc.)	30 minutes per 1 inch of thickness

CRAFTING WITH YOUR CONVECTION OVEN

Many craft tasks can be speeded up if you let your convection oven help. When any craft object has to be air dried, it can be done faster in a turned-on convection oven with the temperature control set at "Off" or "0." *Do not* use your oven as a drying chamber for craft projects if the temperature control cannot be set at "Off" or "0."

PAPIER-MÂCHÉ

Papier-mâché, whether it's done by children in grade school or adults with sophisticated tastes, always provokes the same question: When will it be dry? It can take days, especially during humid weather, to thoroughly dry a papier-mâché object. Placing it in a convection oven with air flow on and the temperature set at "Off" or "0" can shorten that time considerably. Keep an eye on papier-mâché objects while they dry to make sure drying is not too fast, which could cause warping, especially of thin objects.

PAINTED OR GLUED OBJECTS

When drying painted or glued objects (such as models, dollhouse furniture, wooden Christmas ornaments) in a convection oven, it is important to remember that they should be small enough to enter the oven easily and not so lightweight that they will be blown around the oven cavity by the circulating air. The oven should be perfectly clean and free of crumbs, lint or dust, as these can end up sticking to wet surfaces and ruining your project.

GUIDELINES FOR CONVECTION-DRYING CRAFTS OBJECTS

● The object should fit in the oven with at least one inch of air space all around.
● Place the object directly on the rack and slide the rack into the oven so the object is centered.
● If the object doesn't balance well on the rack, place it on an aluminum baking sheet, ideally one just large enough to hold the object.
● In the case of painted objects, paint the bottom first and dry inverted in the oven. Then paint the top and sides and dry again in the oven. This will prevent the paint from getting on the oven rack.

DOUGH SCULPTURE: ART FROM YOUR OVEN

One of the most creative and lasting crafts for children and adults alike is dough sculpture. The basic mixture is as easy to make as a packaged cake mix and contains only three ingredients, all found in the kitchen: flour, salt and water.

This dough is not meant for eating but for making Christmas ornaments, wall decorations, nameplates, jewelry, plaques or any other item your imagination can conjure up. In the instructions that follow, everything except the optional finishing varnish can be found in the kitchen. Dough sculpture is truly a cook's craft because so many of the techniques used are cooking techniques. The same fingers that squeeze a garlic press can fashion hair for a gingerbread man; the same hand that rolls the pizza cutter through gooey mozzarella can roll out free-form initials. And the same delicate touch needed to decorate a puff pastry creation is needed to apply decorations to a dough sculpture.

A convection oven can help dough sculptors achieve three different finishes: white and dull (air-dried finish), brown and dull (baked finish) and brown and glossy (baked with egg yolk glaze).

Instructions for these finishes are given here along with the Basic Sculpting Dough recipe and directions for making cookie cutter and free-form dough sculpture ornaments.

BASIC SCULPTING DOUGH

2 cups all-purpose flour
1 cup salt
Food coloring (optional)
1 cup water

Combine flour and salt in large mixing bowl. To color dough, add food coloring to water, then knead in additional food coloring, if desired. Gradually add water and mix to form ball; for best results, mix dough by hand. If dough is too dry, add more water a teaspoon at a time; if dough is sticky, add flour a teaspoon at a time. Knead dough on lightly floured surface 7 to 10 minutes or until dough is smooth and firm. If dough sticks, knead in more flour. Wrap in plastic bag and keep in refrigerator until ready to use. Can be stored in refrigerator up to 5 days before using.

THE TOOLS YOU'LL NEED

Rolling pin	Cookie cutters
Sharp knife	Toothpicks
Pizza cutter	Paper clips
Garlic press	Fork
Pastry brush	Butter knife
Pencil	Baking sheets
Spatula	

To Make Cookie Cutter and Free-Form Decorations (see illustrations): Shape the dough into thick patty. Roll out on a lightly floured surface as you would roll out pie crust. The dough should be slightly less than 1/4 inch thick. Use cookie cutters or a sharp knife to cut shapes from dough. (Let your cookie cutters inspire your designs.) If the dough sticks, dip the cutters in flour and shake off the excess before cutting

each shape. Transfer shapes to baking sheet. After the basic shapes have been cut, gather up the scraps and roll out again to a thickness of 1/8 inch or less. With cookie cutters or a knife or pizza cutter, cut decorative shapes such as boots for a gingerbread man or an apron for a gingerbread lady. Use bits of dough to make eyes and mouths. Force a lump of dough through a garlic press to make hair or a beard or grass. To apply decorations to shapes or to join two pieces together, moisten both edges with water using a fingertip or small pastry brush and press the pieces together gently but firmly. Use a dull knife blade, fork, toothpick or similar tools to give texture to the dough. The tines of a fork can make fingers on a gingerbread man; the end of a knife blade can make a wing shape on a bird. If the decoration is meant to hang, use a toothpick or cake tester to poke a hole near the top edge, or press a paper clip to the back top edge of the object to make a loop; thread string or fishline through the hole or loop to hang. The hole will close slightly during baking, so make it large enough in the beginning. Convection air-dry or bake to finish by one of the following methods.

Convection Air-Dried Finish (white and stonelike): Place one or more baking sheets of dough sculpture pieces in the convection oven. Turn the temperature control to "Off" or "0"; turn on the oven, setting the timer for maximum time. Allow the dough to dry in the oven until it is rigid enough to remove from the baking sheet, about four to six hours. (You will have to reset the timer during this period.) Gently slide a thin spatula under pieces to loosen them. The bottoms will be moist and soft. Place pieces on a cooling rack or directly on the oven rack, depending on the technique you wish to use to dry them.

Dough sculptures can finish air drying at room temperature or by a combination of air drying and convection drying. To air dry at room temperature, place pieces on cooling rack and let sit at room temperature until they are white and rock-hard. This should take about 48 hours. To dry by a combination of still air and convection air, place pieces directly on oven rack and alternate periods of air drying and convection drying. Periods do not have to be equal; drying in oven two hours, then out of oven four to six hours will hasten drying time considerably. This alternating method is faster than straight air drying; how much faster depends upon the humidity in the air, the temperature of the kitchen and the size and thickness of the dough sculpture pieces. When pieces are completely dry (white and stonelike), coat with clear shellac or acrylic sealer for a permanent finish.

Convection-Baked Finish (brown and dull): Set the convection oven temperature control at 325°F. Place one or more baking sheets of dough sculpture in oven; turn on the oven. There is no need to preheat oven, but the pieces will bake faster if the oven is preheated. Bake about 30 minutes for each 1/4 inch of thickness. The pieces should turn light brown and rock-hard. To speed drying, remove the baking sheet and place objects directly on the oven rack after they have become rigid enough to move, about 20 minutes. If a bubble or puff appears, reduce the oven temperature by 25 degrees and deflate the bubble by poking with a pin or toothpick. The pieces must be rock-hard before applying finishing coat. To prevent moisture from affecting your sculpture, paint on all sides and edges with clear shellac or acrylic sealer.

Egg Yolk Finish (brown and glossy): Follow the Convection-Baked Finish instructions above with the following modification: After the pieces have baked 10 minutes, remove from oven and brush with a glaze made by mixing one egg yolk and one tablespoon water. Repeat brushing as often as desired during baking to deepen color. Apply one or two coats of clear shellac or acrylic sealer.

To Make Plaques: Use white glue or other hobby glue to glue dough sculpture pieces to finished wooden plaques. Follow glue instructions for best results. Set glue in air flow of convection oven, if desired (see page 142).

To Make Jewelry: Glue pin backs, earring backs or cuff links to dough sculpture pieces with white glue or other hobby glue. Follow glue instructions. Place objects in air flow of convection oven to set glue, if desired (see page 142).

To Make Christmas Ornaments: Thread string, decorative cord or "invisible" fishline through holes or loops in dough sculpture pieces.

DEHYDRATING

In the most basic terms, dehydrating is removing the water from fresh foods. While dehydrating is experiencing a resurgence in popularity today and may seem like a new-fangled idea, it is actually the oldest form of food preservation. Long before canning, refrigerators and freezers came on the scene, people were drying foods by sunlight, a technique that is practical only in warm, sunny climates. Oven dehydrating can be done year-round in all types of climates.

Oven dehydrating should be done at 140° to 150° F. Only a limited number of convection oven models have the capability of maintaining that temperature over a long period of time. *Check your oven's temperature control to see if it includes a setting as low as 150°F and consult your care-and-use manual for specific dehydrating instructions.* If you wish to purchase a convection oven that dehydrates, question the salesperson and read the packaging information before making a selection. Buying a unit with dehydrating capability is a money-saving move if you are serious about drying foods. It will save the expense of purchasing a separate dehydrating appliance, not to mention the savings of counter space. Special dehydrating racks and other accessories are available from oven manufacturers. *Note: dehydrating should be attempted only if your oven's care-and-use manual recommends it and you have the proper special equipment.* Follow the manufacturer's directions.

index

BIOGRAPHICAL NOTES

Caroline Kriz is a freelance writer and food consultant and a former editor of *Sphere* magazine. She holds her bachelor of science degree in home economics from Purdue University and her master of science in journalism from Northwestern University, and has studied in Paris at La Varenne and with food authorities Simone Beck, Jacques Pepin and John Clancy.